# EXPERIENTIAL EXERCISES

# IN

# ORGANIZATIONAL BEHAVIOUR

**CAROL A. SALES**
*Brock University*

**FRANCES A. OWEN**
*Niagara University*

**MARY ANN LESPERANCE**
*Marshall & Company*

Prentice Hall Canada Inc., Scarborough, Ontario

ISBN 0-13-021806-5

Publisher and Editorial Director: Patrick Ferrier
Acquisitions Editor: Mike Ryan
Senior Marketing Manager: Ann Byford
Developmental Editor: Sherry Torchinsky
Production Editor: Mary Ann McCutcheon
Production Coordinator: Janette Lush
Cover Design: Julia Hall, Monica Kompter
Cover Image: Photodisk

3 4 5 DPC 11 10 09

Printed and bound in Canada

## DEDICATION

To    Betty Sales
       and
       Jane and Betty Jean Lavallee  (C.A.S.)

To    F. George-Ann Owen
       and
       In memory of John V. Owen  (F.A.O.)

To    My son, Marshall, for keeping me light-hearted and grounded  (M.A.L.)

# TABLE OF CONTENTS

# PREFACE

Organizational Behaviour is truly a dynamic field of study. These exercises have been developed to introduce students to some of the issues, experiences, and dilemmas that face managers and human resource professionals on a day to day basis. From a constructivist perspective, these experiential exercises will encourage organizational behaviour students to develop their personal perspectives on life in contemporary workplaces. The debriefing activities presented as part of each exercise will further encourage students to become reflective learners.

*Experiential Exercises in Organizational Behaviour* is one of a series of three related books of experiential exercises. The other two are *Experiential Exercises in Human Resource Management* and *Experiential Exercises in Management*. This book has been developed with one eye firmly focused on theory and the other firmly focused on the needs of practitioners. As part of the planning process for this project, a focus group was held in Toronto with HR and senior business professionals from a variety of organizations. They were asked to discuss the major issues facing people in the field today, the skills and competencies they look for in new human resource professionals in the areas of Human Resource Management and Organizational Behaviour, and the pressures that are likely to arise in the foreseeable future. The results of this focus group, combined with literature from the academic and professional sectors, guided our selection of topics.

This book is organized into six parts. The exercises in Part 1 provide an Introduction To Organizational Behaviour In Contemporary Canadian Organizations. This section includes exercises which offer an overview of the nature of contemporary organizations and showcase trends (and fads) in the management of human resources. Topics such as: ethics, social responsibility, outplacement, telecommuting, and the employment contract are included.

Part 2 focuses on Basic Human Processes. Featured topics are: person-job fit, learning, social perception, performance management and human resource development.

Part 3 spotlights the Individual In The Organization. This set of exercises centres around various models of motivation and their applications, reward and recognition programs, redesign of work space to improve productivity, issues in valuing diversity, work-related attitudes, orientation of new hires, mentoring programs, and managing stress.

Part 4 highlights issues related to Group Processes. These exercises focus on: group dynamics and teamwork, interpersonal communication, decision making and problem solving techniques, and organizational citizenship behaviour.

Part 5 focuses on Influencing Others. Topics such as the following are presented in this section: power bases, politics in organizations, competency-based behavioural interviewing techniques, humour as a management tool, and leadership models and their applications.

Part 6 concludes the book with a look at Organizational Processes. Organizational culture, technology, learning organizations, and resistance to change are featured in this set of exercises.

The Instructor's Resource Manual that accompanies this book provides background and support materials that facilitate completion of the exercises.

This book will challenge students to explore the dynamic field of organizational behaviour and the fascinating world of contemporary workplaces. It is our fondest hope that students will have fun learning through these exercises.

# ACKNOWLEDGMENTS

We are very grateful for the help and support of the team at Prentice Hall Canada in particular we would like to thank Sherry Torchinsky and Amber Wallace for their guidance and understanding. We wish to thank the HR and management professionals who shared their experience and concerns with us: Kate Wooten, The Hospital for Sick Children; Marnie Keith-Murray, Keith-Murray Partnership; Brian Flanagan, The Toronto Hospital; Jeff Lee, The Toronto Hospital; Stephen Ryan, UNUM CANADA; Christine Croucher, CIBC; Andrea Waines, Miller Dallas Inc.; and Pete Van Hezewyk, Loyalty Management Group. This book would never have been completed without the skill, good humour and endless energy and patience of Rosalie Velicevic. Her computer skills were invaluable in the completion of this book. We are also grateful to Amanda Oosterveer for the skill, good humour and patience she brought to the project wrap-up. This was truly a team effort which gave us all an opportunity to learn from one another.

Carol Sales wishes to express her gratitude to Frances Owen and Mary Ann Lesperance for their dedication to this book and for their continuing friendship and mentoring. She also wishes to thank Joel J. and Frank B. Samuels and her colleagues at Brock University, especially: Dean Martin Kusy, Ronald McTavish, Mark Thomas, Eli Levanoni, Sharon Broderick, John Barr, Margot Adams-Webber, and Jila Boal.

Frances Owen wishes to thank the other members of writing team, Carol Sales and Mary Ann Lesperance, for a wonderful learning experience. She is also grateful to her colleagues in the College of Education at Niagara University for their encouragement and good humour: Father Daniel O'Leary, Dean of Education, Dr. Robin Erwin, Chair, Drs. Salvatore Pappalardo, Jackie MacFarland, Deborah Erickson, Thomas Sheeran, Paul Vermette, Frank Calzi, Carmelo Sapone, Chandra Foote, Rita Moretti, Alice Blake-Stalker, Jennifer Wilson-Bridgman, and Delar Singh, and to Mary Anne Brown for her patience. Special thanks to Dr. Victor Owen, Sheila Moores, Jim, Julie and Evan Owen and, especially to Joel J. and Frank B. Samuels for keeping her grounded.

Mary Ann Lesperance is ever grateful to Carol Sales and Frances Owen for their leap of faith in asking her to join their team. She wishes to thank her family, professional colleagues, and friends for their input, encouragement, support, patience, and continual belief in her abilities, especially her Mom (Mary Lesperance Hulett), Victoria's parents (Lisa Craig and Peter Van Hezewyk), Brian Flanagan, Cory Hagopian, Mary Knapp, Debbie Lee, Linda Morrison, Gary and Diana Lesperance, Laurie Panchyshyn and the Grey Gables' Ladies, and her Book Club.

# PART 1

# INTRODUCTION TO ORGANIZATIONAL BEHAVIOUR IN CONTEMPORARY CANADIAN ORGANIZATIONS

# 1. LET ME TELL YOU ABOUT MY JOB: ORGANIZATIONAL ART

 **LEARNING OBJECTIVES:**

1.  To serve as an icebreaker for the many experiential exercises to be presented throughout this course.

2.  To provide a vehicle through which you can learn more about work organizations with which you are already somewhat familiar. e.g., co-op placements and summer jobs.

3.  To give you an opportunity to look at your work organization "through a fish-eye lens" and visualize for classmates a sample of the complex interpersonal interactions you have encountered.

4.  To begin your personal journey of integrating course material and your own work experience.

5.  To present an opportunity for you to gain an appreciation of "the bigger picture" of the organizations e.g., the micro and macro issues in people management.

**TYPE OF EXERCISE:**

Small group activities and class-wide discussion

**RELATED CONCEPTS:**

*   Micro and Macro Organizational Behaviour, Organizational Theory, and Design topics:

    *   motivation
    *   communication
    *   stress
    *   conflict and co-operation
    *   leadership and supervision

- control and culture
- human resource management practices
- working environment and quality of work life

 **TIME:** 25 minutes

Small groups will typically require a maximum of 15 minutes to complete discussion, planning and drawing their organizational art. Each group in turn will then display its "creation" and will offer a brief interpretation for the rest of the class. Class discussion will not be held until after all groups have presented their artwork. This is expected to take 2 minutes per group.

Next, the instructor and the class will discuss their interpretations and their reactions to the artwork. This part of the activity could add up to 3 minutes per group.

## BACKGROUND:

Work organizations are everywhere. They come in all shapes and sizes. Some endure short, tortuous existence while others sustain long, prideful organizational lives. Some plot ambitious global treks. Others are content to stay on the home turf. Whatever their mission, size, and global reach, work organizations profoundly affect the lives of those they employ and beyond.

Your first lessons about the inner complexities of work organizations most likely came from overhearing the daily "post-mortem" analyses recounted with a fair bit of animation, if not agitation, by your parents and siblings. Later, while still at school, you may have found yourself experiencing these infamous work organizations as you were hired for part-time jobs or selected for co-op placements.

This exercise will give you the opportunity to share your insights on and feelings about the inner workings of the organization you know best.

David Cherrington[1], from whose work this exercise is adapted, offers the following illustrations as inspiration for your drawings or cartoons:

> A woman who worked in a large bureaucratic organization with rigid rules and procedures caricatured her organization as a large dinosaur sinking in a pool of quicksand which represented the rules. One of her colleagues illustrated the same idea by drawing a picture of an overweight cat entangled in a ball of twine, which represented the rules. A person who worked in the formatting department of an advertising agency wrote the story about a hapless fool who was caught on a treadmill with fire-breathing dragons close behind. A union steward drew a picture of a battle scene between management and union. The company logo or union symbol on the warriors' swords and shields depicted the union's assault against the corporate castle.

 **MATERIALS NEEDED:**

- One sheet of flip chart paper for each small group
- One set of coloured markers (with at least 3 different colours)
- One roll of masking tape

**PROCESS/INSTRUCTIONS:**

1. Your instructor will divide the class into groups of four.

2. Each person in the group will describe one summer job or co-op placement (or other organizational setting) to group members within one minute each. A "fish-eye" view should be encouraged for the description.

3. Within your group, decide on the most interesting workplace and proceed to tell the story by drawing a multi-colour cartoon or writing a metaphor. Your group member who actually experienced this situation will instruct other group members on how best to illustrate it.

4. Your instructor will ask each group in turn to present its cartoon (or metaphor) to the class.

**DEBRIEFING:**

1. What are the common organizational themes depicted in the artwork (e.g., good management practices, bad management practices, the pressures, feelings of success)?

2.    Based on the course outline, or the table of contents of your text, what topics do you
      expect will address the common organizational themes you identified in your answer to
      question 1. above?

3.    What conclusions can be drawn from this exercise with respect to the importance of
      people management skills in today's organizations?

**REFERENCE:**

1.    Cherrington, D. (1989). *Organizational Behavior: The Management of Individual and
      Organizational Performance.* Upper Saddle River, NJ: Prentice-Hall Inc., p. 511.
      Reprinted by permission.

## 2. I'D LIKE YOU TO MEET... :
## INTRODUCTION TO ORGANIZATIONAL BEHAVIOUR

 **LEARNING OBJECTIVES:**

1.      To serve as an icebreaker for this class and course.

2.      To highlight the personal side of organizational behaviour.

3.      To mirror the personal characteristics you most admire in others.

## TYPE OF EXERCISE:

Individual, written assignment and class-wide discussion

## RELATED CONCEPTS:

•        Introduction to organizational behaviour

 **TIME:** 10 minutes

The debriefing for this exercise will typically require 10 minutes of in-class time.

## BACKGROUND:

Different cultures value different personal characteristics. These values tend to be highlighted when introducing someone to another person. This exercise will encourage you to think about the characteristics that you value most.

## PREASSIGNMENT STUDENT PREPARATION:

1.      Outside of class, within the time frame given by your instructor, write a one page (maximum) memo in which you introduce a relative to your Organizational Behaviour

instructor. You may elaborate on only three pieces of information about your relative (name and how you are related don't count in the three). Be sure to put your name on the memo so that your instructor can return the memo directly to you. Hand the memo to your instructor. Rest assured that the memos will be discussed in class only in a global manner and not on an individual basis i.e., no individual memo, student's name, or relative's name will be identified during this exercise.

2.  After your instructor has had a chance to read these memos, she or he will explain more about this writing exercise in class and will return your memo to you.


**DEBRIEFING:**

1.  What kind of information do you think was shared about most of the relatives introduced in the memos? Please explain your answer.

2.  What point was your instructor making by having you do this exercise?

3.  What kind of information was shared in the memos which seems to be unique in some way? What does this teach you?

4.     How important was the occupation of the relatives introduced in the memos?

5.     How central is work in the lives of the relatives introduced in the memos?

6.     What can you deduce about the work values of members of your class from the memos?

# 3. FAD SOUP:
## HOT, COOLING AND COLD MANAGEMENT IDEAS IN CONTEMPORARY CANADIAN ORGANIZATIONS

 **LEARNING OBJECTIVES:**

1. To facilitate your research into recent and current management trends and (what some would call) fads in contemporary Canadian organizations.

2. To help you to develop the necessary skills to be able to evaluate the potential of a myriad of management trends (and fads).

**TYPE OF EXERCISE:**

Small group activities and class-wide discussion

**RELATED CONCEPTS:**

- Organizational behaviour
- Organizational design
- Management

 **TIME:** 50 minutes

Small groups will require 20 minutes to brainstorm, briefly describe and label the popularity and lasting impact of a myriad of management trends and fads. The class-wide discussion to compare the lists developed by each group will take 20 minutes. The debriefing will require an additional 10 minutes.

**BACKGROUND:**

As you read newspapers, journals and the wide selection of business books available every year, and as you listen to radio, watch television and surf the Internet, you are bombarded by new management ideas and programs that are being tried out in organizations. For managers who are investing substantial human and financial resources to implement these ideas and programs, sorting the wheat from the chaff can be challenging. Differentiating between passing fads and viable trends that will positively impact an organization's bottom line is the challenge facing line managers and HR professionals in the 21st century.

This exercise will give you an opportunity to learn about contemporary management ideas and programs that Canadian organizations are using and, more importantly, to evaluate critically the long and short term value of these ideas and programs.

 **MATERIALS NEEDED:**

- Four sheets of flip chart paper and one marker for each small group
- One flip chart, pad and marker for use by the instructor
- One roll of masking tape

## PROCESS/INSTRUCTIONS:

1.  Your instructor will divide the class into small groups. Your group will be given four sheets of flip chart paper and a marker. Elect one group member as a recorder.

2.  Brainstorm a list of management ideas and programs which are regarded, or have been regarded in recent years, as trends or fads in organizations aimed at increasing productivity (efficiency and/or effectiveness), increasing profitability, and improving the quality of worklife for employees. Your instructor will identify one current trend as a sample to get you started. Be sure to record a brief description of each management idea or program you list.

3.  In round-robin fashion, your instructor will ask each recorder to name and describe one management idea or program identified by his or her group. Your instructor will then write the names and descriptions on the flip chart at the front of the room. A number will be assigned to each program. When your instructor deems this master list to be complete, he or she will tape these flip chart sheets up across the front of the room.

4.  The recorder for each group will take a new page on the flip chart paper. At this point, the flip chart paper should be turned sideways (landscape) to gain the maximum width of page. This page will be divided into five columns e.g., the first column from the left will list the numbers assigned to each particular management idea or program (see Step 3. above) and will be labelled "Idea/Program", the second column will estimate the popularity of each idea or program (using a single letter of the alphabet) and will be labelled "Popularity" (see Step 5. below), the third column from the left will be somewhat wider than columns 1 and 2 and will be labelled "Rationale" i.e., rationale for your popularity rating of each idea or program, the fourth column from the left will estimate

the lasting impact on organizational effectiveness over time of each idea or program i.e., lasting impact or little impact, and finally, the fifth column from the left will be labelled "Rationale" i.e., rationale for your rating of the likely impact on organizational effectiveness over time.

5.  With the guidance of group recorder, complete the new chart established in Step 4. above. Estimate the popularity of each idea or program using the following labels: "H" for "hot" (a leading edge program), "L" for "lukewarm" (losing its popularity) and "C" for "cold" (generally out of favour today) and also label your estimate of the long term impact of each idea or program using the following labels: "T" for "trend" (true impact on organizational effectiveness over time) or "F" for "fad" (popular now but not likely to impact on organizational effectiveness over time).

6.  Your instructor will remove the posted lists of ideas and programs from the front of the room. Each recorder will now post his or her completed chart across the front of the room. Your instructor will guide your class in a discussion of the simlarities and differences in the rating given to each program (or a selected number of programs).

**DEBRIEFING:**

1.  What is the difference between a management "trend" and a "fad"? Give two examples of each. Be sure to include your rationale for each example.

2.  Why are there so many fads sweeping through contemporary Canadian organizations?

3.	Did the popularity rating (i.e., hot, lukewarm or cold) for some programs differ across groups in the class exercise? How do you explain this?

4.	What are the drawbacks of management's "fadsurfing" (so called by one writer)?

5.	How can management avoid the pitfalls of investing in very popular but passing fads?

**FOLLOW-UP ACTIVITIES:**

1.	Be prepared to repeat this exercise near the end of the course (if desired by your instructor) in order to discuss the trends and fads that have developed in the interim.

2.	Make your projections on what will be the next "big trend(s)" and the next "big fad(s)" based on your reading of the popular press and other media and your surfing of the web?

# 4. TOTALLY RAD:
## A MEDIA SCAVENGER HUNT PORTFOLIO OF POSITIVE AND FUN TRENDS IN CONTEMPORARY ORGANIZATIONS

 **LEARNING OBJECTIVES:**

1.      To give you an opportunity to search the media for "signs of the times" in contemporary work organizations.

2.      To heighten your awareness of the many new and positive changes which are affecting the workforce.

3.      To have fun doing this assignment and to create a lasting memory of this course.

**TYPE OF EXERCISE:**

Individual portfolio and class presentations

**RELATED CONCEPTS:**

*   Organizational trends
*   Organizational culture
*   Changing workplace demographics
*   Managerial practices
*   Leadership
*   Motivation

 **TIME:** 10 minutes (per student presentation distributed throughout the course)

Individual students will given a maximum of 10 minutes (or a different time limit as authorized by your instructor) to present their portfolio to the class. Your instructor will draw up a schedule of available time slots that run from the middle of the course to the end.

## BACKGROUND:

There's no doubt that contemporary organizations are reeling from the dizzying twirl of change that has swept through in the last decade or so. The media, it seems, has profiled the negative side effects with painful persistence. But there is another side - a positive side to changes flooding into contemporary organizations. The younger generations which have entered the workforce over the last 10 years or so are making their presence felt and are changing the face of work in many positive ways.

This exercise will give you an opportunity to look at the interesting and fun side of working in contemporary organizations.

## PREASSIGNMENT STUDENT PREPARATION:

In the first quarter of this course, your instructor will outline the requirements of this assignment for you. In essence, you will work alone outside of class to complete a portfolio of media items to show your understanding of the positive changes that are changing the face of Canadian workplaces. For a period of a few weeks, you will be searching all forms of media e.g., daily newspapers, popular business magazines, recent movies, news documentaries, televison business programs, and the Internet. Your end product, or as HR professionals call it your "deliverable" will be a collage of media items amassed in one well-designed portfolio which you will present to the class in a 10 minute time slot sometime after the mid-point of this course. Your instructor will assign the time slots (specific class day and 10 minute time slot) by lottery in the first few weeks of this course.

Your portfolio will be entitled: "The changing face of work" and must contain (at minimum) the following (unless otherwise directed by your instructor):

- five cartoons representing at least three different cartoon strips and your commentary on each;
- two references to a movie with your commentary;
- the web addresses and your summary of the sites of three Canadian companies with interesting and fun organizational cultures;
- three newspaper articles and your commentary on each;
- three articles from three different popular business magazines with your commentary on each; and
- two summaries of a Canadian business televison program (aired between six months before this course started and today) e.g., CBC's Venture, The National Magazine, or Culture Shock.

In addition you might want to approach several organizations in your community to obtain a copy of interesting promotional material to display in your portfolio. Some organizations might even lend you a copy of their promotional video.

Remember your overall goal in this assignment is to showcase your knowledge of the positive side of the changing place of work. To make a final selection on any item for your portfolio, ask yourself if this item would have been likely to have appeared in the media five years ago and if this item is workplace-related, interesting and fun. If your answer is "yes", include the item in your portfolio. If your answer is "no", forget about this item. If you have fun amassing this portfolio, your classmates will enjoy listening to your presentation.

## PROCESS/INSTRUCTIONS:

Present your portfolio to the class in your time slot (drawn earlier in the course by lottery).

## FOLLOW-UP ACTIVITIES:

1. Invite HR professionals and other leaders and managers from organizations in your community to hear and comment on the portfolio presentations.

2. Assemble a class portfolio that contains the very best items from all the portfolios and offer to present it as a part of your school's next Open House for the public or to take it to local high schools as a part of your school's high school recruitment program.

3. Keep your portfolio intact to take with you to job interviews to showcase your understanding of contemporary workplaces.

## 5. WHAT'S HOT AND WHAT'S NOT FOR CANADIAN 2K ORGANIZATIONS: ORGANIZATIONAL BEHAVIOUR IN THE NEWS

 **LEARNING OBJECTIVES:**

1.      To expose you to the up-to-the-minute breaking news in the North American popular business media e.g. *Canadian Business, Fast Company, Fortune, Forbes, Inc, The Globe and Mail, The National Post*, etc.

2.      To highlight the complex micro and macro issues facing CEOs, managers and workers as they enter the 21$^{st}$ century.

3.      To direct your searches for "best practice" organizations.

4.      To provide you with an opportunity to begin to amass a kit-bag of models of successful new management programs.

5.      To encourage you to view management trends and fads in a critical fashion.


## TYPE OF EXERCISE:

Two oral class reports and a written report prepared by an individual, a pair or a small group of students describing issues facing a contemporary Canadian organization featured in the media. Data on the organization will be drawn from articles in business publications. A preliminary oral report will be given in class within two weeks of the initial assignment and the final oral report and submission of the written report will take place near the end of the course.


## RELATED CONCEPTS:

*       Micro and macro organizational behaviour
*       Systems view of organizations

**TIME:** Reports to be presented in several different classes.

Preliminary oral report should be less than 4 minutes for each reporting unit. The final oral report should not exceed 10 minutes for each reporting unit. The written report is due at the end of the class in which the final oral report is made.

## BACKGROUND/INTRODUCTION:

This exercise is designed to bring the "real world" of Canadian business into the classroom. As you review the business literature during this exercise, you will become familiar with information sources you will use long after this course has ended. You will also become aware of up-to-the-minute issues facing Canadian organizations as they deal with the process of change in response to shifting markets, environment, and legislative pressures.

 **MATERIALS NEEDED:**

• Two sets of index cards (two different colours)

## PROCESS/INSTRUCTIONS:

1.   Your instructor will announce the size of the reporting unit (i.e., individual, pair or small group), the date for the oral reports, and the deadline for final oral report and the written report.

2.   Your instructor will hold a "lottery" for sources e.g., *Canadian Business, Business Week, Fast Company, Forbes, Inc, The Globe and Mail, The National Post, etc.*, in which each reporting unit is expected to search for a company that has undergone radical change lately or is contemplating radical change. Oral and written report due dates will be written on each index card. Each reporting unit draws an index card.

3.   Reporting units are given 5 minutes in which they may swap index cards with other consenting reporting units. After the swap period, each reporting unit prints the name of each member on the index card and hands the card back to your instructor.

4.   Your instructor will photocopy the index cards (five per sheet) and either post these or hand out copies of the lists to jog your memory on the details and dates of the assignment.

5.   Please read the section entitled: Assignment Instructions (on the next two pages) and complete the assignment as directed.

# ASSIGNMENT INSTRUCTIONS

<u>Sources must be dated on or after, January 1, 1998</u>. You are asked to apply course material directly to a contemporary organization. Each reporting group will choose one article which outlines some new development in the management of a particular organization. You will be asked to register, and thus reserve, your choice of article soon in. The lottery will determine from which publication each reporting unit must draw its article. Source publications, determined by the lottery, include: *The Globe and Mail - Managing Page, Fast Company, Business Week, Forbes, Inc, Fortune, Canadian Business,* and *The National Post.*

This assignment has three parts, namely: a preliminary oral report to the class, a final oral report to the class and a final written report. The time limit for each preliminary oral report will be <u>four minutes</u> for each reporting unit. The time limit for final oral reports will be 10 minutes (for each reporting unit). The following information will be reported to class on the chosen article/company.

## PRELIMINARY ORAL REPORT:

1. A very brief sketch (a few sentences only) of the content of the article;
2. Why you chose this article for this assignment (i.e., relationship to the course material).

## FINAL ORAL REPORT

1. A very brief sketch (a few sentences only) of the content of the article as a reminder for the class;
2. A quick sketch of the "nature of the business" and "key success factors" for this type of organization;
3. An overview of the application of course material to the article/company;
4. Your conclusions with regard to all aspects of the changes being made in the organization and the methods the organization is using to implement these changes; and
5. Your speculation on the future of this company given these changes.

## WRITTEN REPORT

The third part of this assignment is the written report.  This report is due immediately after the final oral report is made in class. There will be a page limit of 4 "typed" pages.  Be sure to attach one copy of your source article marked "for educational purposes" to the written report. The following headings must be addressed:

1.      Summary of the Source Article;
2.      Nature of Such a Business for your company;
3.      Key Success Factors of Such a Business for your company;
4.      Direct Application of Course Theory/Concepts;
5.      Evaluation of Organizational Change(s) and Prognosis.

---

## DEBRIEFING:

1.      With which three companies' change efforts were you most impressed? Please explain your answer.

2.      With which three companies' change efforts were you least impressed? Please explain your answer.

3.      What trends could you identify (across all of the reports given in class) with respect to "people management" in contemporary Canadian organizations?

# 6. SORRY, BUT YOUR SERVICES ARE NO LONGER REQUIRED: CHOOSING AN OUTPLACEMENT SERVICE PROVIDER TO SUPPORT DOWNSIZING

 **LEARNING OBJECTIVES:**

1.  To highlight the role outplacement can play to support downsizing in contemporary organizations.

2.  To investigate the various services offered by outplacement organizations.

3.  To provide you with the opportunity to compare and contrast a number of contemporary outplacement organizations.


**TYPE OF EXERCISE:**

Individual Internet research, small group activities and class-wide discussion

**RELATED CONCEPTS:**

*   HR planning
*   HR and organizational trend analysis
*   Downsizing
*   Termination of employment
*   Legal issues in HR

 **TIME:** 55 minutes

Sharing the yield from your Internet search with your group and reading the scenario will typically require 15 minutes. The assessment and final recommendation on your assigned outplacement organization will take 10 minutes. The class presentations will require 15 minutes. Finally, the vote and the debriefing will require an additional 15 minutes.

## BACKGROUND:

The nasty 90s will long be remembered by many, including middle- and upper-level managers, as the era of downsizing and termination. Some organizations offer terminated employees an assistance program called "outplacement counselling" to help them to find alternate employment elsewhere. Many companies have chosen to outsource their outplacement services to outside specialists, such as: KPMG, Drake Beam Morin (DBM), Mainstream Access, Miller Dallas, Right Associates, R.W. Caldwell Associates Inc. and Morgan & Banks. The costs to employers of providing such outplacement services vary dramatically across outplacement organizations depending on the number of service elements provided to clients i.e., self-assessment and counselling, job search skills including résumé writing, work space, office equipment such as: computers, fax machine, photocopier, clerical assistance, mail services, information on the labour market and trend analysis.[1]

This exercise will give you the opportunity to learn about the role of outplacement in downsizing and termination and about the various service elements offered to clients by outsourced outplacement organizations.

 **MATERIALS NEEDED:**

- Seven 3" x 5" index cards for the outplacement organization lottery (supplied by your instructor)
- One sheet of flip chart paper and one marker for each of the seven small groups
- One roll of masking tape

## PREASSIGMENT STUDENT PREPARATION:

1. Before the class in which you will be completing this exercise, visit the web sites of the following organizations who offer outplacement services:

    - Mainstream Access Corp. (http://www.mainstreamaccess.com/)
    - KPMG Canada (http://www.kpmg.ca/es/home.htm)
    - R.W. Caldwell Associates, Inc.(http://www.rwcaldwell.com/)
    - Right Associates (http://www.rsv.com/catalog.htm)
    - Miller Dallas Inc. (http://www.millerdallas.com/)
    - Morgan & Banks (http://www.morganbanks.com.au/index.htm)
    - Drake Beam Morin Canada (http://www.dbmcanada.com/)

    For each organization, please note the following information: location of the organization, range of outplacement/career transition services offered and client base (employee/management level). Please bring your notes to class.

2. Visit the web site of Human Resources Development Canada's Human Resource Office For Employers (http://www.hroe.org/t3.cfm?catnum=10&subcatnum=57&lang=EN&prov_code=ON). At this site, you will find links to two articles by William S. Frank, President of CareerLab entitled: 1. Costly Outplacement Mistakes Can Hinder Downsizing Efforts and 2. How Outplacement Prevents Lawsuits. Please read each article and make notes. Please bring your notes to class. (For your information, CareerLab's web site is http://www.careerlab.com).

**PROCESS/INSTRUCTIONS:**

1. Please read the following scenario:

   *You are a Director, Employee Relations for a large hospital in Toronto. As a result of recent restructuring, you are eliminating 3 director-level positions. The average annual salary for a director-level position is $85 000. You have been asked by the Chief Operating Officer (COO) to investigate a number of large outplacement organizations. You are to review the services offered and to recommend an interim list of three providers for outplacement for these terminated persons. All three of these individuals are based in or around the Toronto area. All have between 8 to 15 years experience in hospital administration. Two of the three would be willing to relocate for other opportunities.*

2. Your instructor will assign you to one of seven small groups. Within your group, share the information you gathered during your Internet search on the outplacement organizations and review the two articles written by William Frank of CareerLab as assigned in the PREASSIGNMENT STUDENT PREPARATION section above.

3. Your instructor will assign one of the seven outplacement organizations to each group by asking a volunteer from each group to participate in a lottery. For your organization, make a list of outplacement services that this particular organization could offer to your three terminated senior hospital administrators. Record the list on a sheet of flip chart paper. Consider what cost information you would want from the organization and the implications of the location of your outplacement organizations. Note this information on your sheet of flip chart paper. Make a decision as to whether or not you would recommend this organization as a potential provider for the three senior administrators (pending cost information, of course!) and note the final rationale offered by your group. Indicate your decision by writing either "Recommended" or "Not Recommended" on the bottom of the flip chart paper.

4. Your instructor will ask each group in turn to present its flip chart summary and rationale for the final decision for its particular outplacement organization. A representative of each group will tape its summary on the chalkboard at the front of the classroom.

5.      Your instructor will ask you to vote for your top three choices of "best fit" outplacement organizations i.e., which of the three organizations you would want to continue to investigate before you write your report to your COO.

**DEBRIEFING:**

1.      Why do companies hire outplacement organizations?

2.      How could outplacement prevent lawsuits?

3.      What some of the "outplacement mistakes" that have been made by companies in their haste to downsize?

4.      What are the various types of services that outplacement organizations offer terminated employees? Upon what factors did you base your "top three outplacement organizations" decision?

5.      Should you recommend the same outplacement service package and the same provider to all three of your terminated hospital adminstrators? Please explain your answer.

6.      Should a company which is in a downsizing/restructuring mode provide outplacement services to all levels of staff? Please explain your answer.

**FOLLOW-UP ACTIVITIES:**

1.      Contact local large organizations who have undergone restructuring in recent years and ask if they utilize(d) an outplacement organization for terminated staff or if they offer(ed) outplacement services to staff as an in-house program.

2.      Choose your number one choice from the class top three list of the outplacement organizations for the Toronto hospital scenario and draft a report to your COO. Be sure to include your recommendation for the types of services you propose to purchase from the outplacement organization. Attempt to discover the cost of your recommendation for the hospital.

**REFERENCE:**

1.      Dessler, G., Cole, N. and Sutherland, V. (1999). *Human Resources Management In Canada*. Canadian Seventh Edition, Scarborough, Ont: Prentice Hall Canada, p. 188.

# 7. HR PROFESSIONALS WITH A GLOBAL REACH: A COMPETENCY MODEL FOR HR PROFESSIONALS WITH WORLDWIDE RESPONSIBILITIES

 **LEARNING OBJECTIVES:**

1.     To facilitate your discovery and review of contemporary HR competency models.

2.     To increase your awareness of the challenges which confront HR professionals in a global company.

3.     To give you the opportunity to learn about the required competencies for HR professionals in a global company.

4.     To give you information about the assimilation, training and development of HR professionals in a global company.

## TYPE OF EXERCISE:

Individual Internet Research, small group activities and class-wide discussion

## RELATED CONCEPTS:

- Global HR
- Competencies and skills
- HR and organizational trend analysis
- HR development
- Globalization
- Cultural differences
- Cross-cultural training

 **TIME:** 60 minutes

Small groups will typically require 15 minutes for sharing the results of their Internet research with regard to the two assigned HR competency models and for choosing a third model. Five minutes will be needed to share the IBM HR information within the groups. The crafting of a fourth model is expected to take 15 minutes. The class presentations of the fourth model and rationale will take 15 minutes. The debriefing will require an additional 10 minutes.

## BACKGROUND:

According to one human resources association [1], an HR competency model "is a vision of the proficiencies needed by the HR professional to compete and contribute successfully." Another HR association[2] says that "competency models have become a dramatic resource in refocusing people on what it takes to succeed in today's workplace."

This exercise will give you an opportunity to research and extend some HR Competency Models which are available to you on the Internet.

## PREASSIGNMENT STUDENT PREPARATION:

1.      Before the class in which you will completing this exercise, search the Internet for examples of HR Competency Models. To get you started, please visit the following two web sites and review the HR Competency Model and background material presented: http://www.linkageinc.com/ghri/competency.htm and http://www.nehra.org/meeting/prof/model.htm. Continue to search the Internet to find at least one other HR Competency Model. Study the HR Competency Models with a view to understanding what the state-of-the-art HR function in a global corporation might look like.

2.      Further, before the class in which you will be completing this exercise, visit the web site of IBM (and IBM Canada linked to the IBM home site) at: http://www.ibm.com/. Explore the site with the view to understanding the HR function in this well-known global company. Be sure also to visit following IBM pages: http://www.empl.ibm.com/html/working_humanrcrs.html (a overview of the HR function); http://www.cybrblu.ibm.com/jobs/hr.html (a more extensive overview of the structure and operations of the HR function at IBM including socialization and professional development opportunities for HR new-hires); and http://www.cybrblu.ibm.com/jobs/cjobhr-1.html (an overview of full-time and co-op HR jobs at IBM). Please make notes on your visits to these sites and bring your notes to class.

 **MATERIALS NEEDED:**

- Four sheets of flip chart paper and one marker for each small group.
- One roll of masking tape.

## PROCESS/INSTRUCTIONS:

1. Your instructor will divide the class into small groups. Within your group, share and discuss briefly the HR competency models you discovered as part of your Internet research in preparation for this class. Draw out a large-scale representation of the two HR competency models you were asked to find in the PREASSIGNMENT STUDENT PREPARATION section above on flip chart paper (one model on each of two sheets of paper).

2. Each person in your group will present the third model that he or she found on the Internet. Your group will choose the one best of these third models and will draw this model out on a third sheet of flip chart paper.

3. Share and discuss what you learned as a result of your Internet search about the HR function at IBM, a large well-known global company.

4. Your group will now take the role of the corporate HR team in a global company (such as IBM). You have been asked by the head of your unit, the VP, HR to craft an HR Competency Model using three such models (see Steps 1. And 2. above) as a point of departure for your task. Your unit has been asked to concentrate in particular on the globalized nature of your company. Within your small group, design an HR Competency Model that would be useful for your corporate HR professionals. Be sure to tape the three models side by side for inspiration on a wall or chalkboard near where your group is working. Draw this model out in large-scale on a fourth sheet of flip chart paper and make notes on your rationale for the model.

5. Your instructor will ask each group to present its HR Competency Model in turn.

**DEBRIEFING:**

1.  What are the competencies necessary for an HR professional who is part of the corporate HR team in a large global company? Please give your rationale for including each competency.

2.  What are the challenges which confront HR professionals who are part of the corporate HR team?

3.  How does IBM assimilate, train and develop its newly hired HR professionals?

4.  What should HR professionals in the corporate HR unit know about cultural differences? How will they acquire this knowledge?

**REFERENCES:**

1. The Northeast Human Resources Association;
   http://www.nehra.org/meetings/prof/model.htm

2. The International Personnel Association; http://www.ipma-hr.org/training/pd.html

# 8. THE ANATOMY OF TWO TRAGEDIES:
## EXAMINING TWO CANADIAN BUSINESSES FOR ETHICS VIOLATIONS

 **LEARNING OBJECTIVES:**

1.      To give you experience in analyzing the roots of an ethical crisis in an organization.

2.      To increase your sensitivity to the impact of ethics violations.


## TYPE OF EXERCISE:

Small group activities and class-wide discussion


## RELATED CONCEPTS:

*       Ethics
*       Group decision making
*       Groupthink

 **TIME:** 45 minutes


Small groups will typically require 20 minutes to consolidate their list of ethics violations. The two group representatives will need 15 minutes in total to give their feedback. The debriefing will require an additional 10 minutes.

## BACKGROUND:

Westray. Bre-X. The mere mention of these now defunct organizations conjures painful memories for millions of Canadians. In both cases, hope for success deteriorated into tragic disaster. In each case, the road to disaster was littered with questionable decisions and alleged violations of accepted business ethics.

This exercise will give you the opportunity to examine the human cost of the apparent ethics violations in these historic Canadian cases.

## PREASSIGNMENT STUDENT PREPARATION:

1.      Your instructor will assign the Westray case to half the class and the Bre-X case to the other half of the class. Each group will be divided into five-member work groups. The task of each group is to research the pattern of alleged ethical violations that led to the downfall of each company and the tragic losses of all those associated with them. Each group will prepare a list of questionable decisions that were made by the management of each company and the factors that contributed to these decisions. Bring these lists to the class in which you will be completing this exercise.

2.      For the group focusing on the Westray mine disaster, you may wish to start your research with the following web sites:

   - Westray investigation was botched, former prosecutor argues in memo (http://www.ottawacitizen.com/national/981217/2110651.html);
   - Westray Coal Mine Disaster (http://www.alts.net/ns1625/wraymenu.html);
   - Westray Mine Public Inquiry Commission (http://www.alts.net/ns1625/wrpi99a.html);
   - Gerald Wilde's article entitled Risk awareness and risk acceptance at the Westray Coal mine (http://pavlov.psyc.queensu.ca/faculty/wilde/westray.html).

3.      For the groups focusing on the Bre-X scandal, you may wish to consider starting your search at CANOE's archive site entitled: The Bre-X Saga (http://www.canoe.ca/MoneyBreXSaga/home.html).

## PROCESS/INSTRUCTIONS:

1.      The groups that researched the Westray Mine disaster will sit together and the groups that researched the Bre-X scandal will sit together. Each of the two integrated groups will meet together to pool the information gathered and to create a common list of apparent ethical violations.

2.      Your instructor will give each group a section of the classroom chalkboard on which to list the apparent ethics violations perpetrated in each case.

3.      Each group of the two integrated groups will appoint one person to present the findings of the group to the class.

## DEBRIEFING:

1.      Discuss the similarities and differences in the apparent ethical violations perpetrated by managers in each company. What factors contributed to these apparent violations?

2.      At what points in each case were there missed opportunities to prevent ethics violations? What could have been done by managers at each of these decision points that might have averted disaster?

## FOLLOW-UP ACTIVITIES:

1.      Check your local newspaper and business magazines for discussion of other business stories with ethical implications.

2.      Invite an ethics specialist from your college or university to join in your discussion of the Westray and Bre-X cases to offer another viewpoint on these tragedies.

# 9. THE DOING WELL AND DOING GOOD TWINS: UNDERSTANDING THE PUSH AND PULL OF CORPORATE SOCIAL RESPONSIBILITY AT HOME AND ABROAD FOR CANADIAN COMPANIES

 **LEARNING OBJECTIVES:**

1. To heighten your awareness of the increasing scope and importance of corporate social responsibility for contemporary Canadian corporations as they do business at home and in developing countries.

2. To give you the opportunity to learn about trends in corporate social responsibility in Canada.

3. To facilitate your review of recent research findings on corporate social responsibility in Canadian companies.

4. To present you with the challenge of identifying the "Top Performing Company In Corporate Social Responsibility " doing business in Canada today.

**TYPE OF EXERCISE:**

Individual Internet research, small group activities, and class-wide discussion

**RELATED CONCEPTS:**

- Corporate social responsibility
- Community relations
- Sustainable development
- Corporate social responsibility in developing countries
- Consumer behaviour

**TIME:** 60 minutes

Small groups will typically require 15 minutes for the initial discussion about corporate social responsibility. The report to the class on the key points of the discussion will take 10 minutes. The sharing of the information on the achievements of the companies researched on the Internet and the reaching of consensus on the one top performer will require 10 minutes each. The class report on the top performers and the vote will require an additional 15 minutes.

## BACKGROUND:

According to the Canadian Centre for Business in the Community, corporate social responsibility "refers to the corporation's overall relationship with stakeholders and includes elements of: financial and ethical performance, environmental stewardship, creation and maintenance of employment, investment in community outreach and Human Resource Management."[1] In the late 1990s, the Conference Board of Canada and Human Resources Development Canada (HRDC) launched their Corporate Social Responsibility (CSR) initiative. "The CSR Initiative is a multiphase project that will: identify best practices in the management of community investment and related human resource practices, identify management practices and functions that form the basis upon which a corporate citizenship program is developed, and identify benchmarks to measure the impact, benefit and effectiveness of community investments and related human resources practices and explore forms of recognition that companies would support and value."[2]

At the heart of the CSR Initative is a group of 22 companies who agreed "to participate in the in-depth interviews that form the core research element of the Initiative."[3] The CSR Initiative and a number of other current research projects are valuable tools for understanding the changing face and increasing importance of corporate social responsibility for Canadian companies.

This exercise will give you the opportunity to deepen your knowledge of the key roles played by corporate social responsibility in the way Canadian companies do business at home and abroad.

 **MATERIALS NEEDED:**

* One sheet of flip chart paper and one marker for each small group
* One small piece of paper (ballot form) for each student (supplied by your instructor)
* One roll of masking tape

## PREASSIGNMENT STUDENT PREPARATION:

1.  Visit the web site of the Canadian Centre For Business in the Community (Conference Board of Canada) at http://www2.conferenceboard.ca/ and click on the "Corporate Responsibility" button. Please explore the site to answer the following questions:

    - What are the factors in the Canadian external environment that are impacting on corporate social responsibility?
    - What are the trends in corporate social responsibility in Canada?
    - Which companies are invited members on the Best Practices Benchmark Group in the CSR Initative?
    - How important is corporate social responsibility to Canadian consumers? Cite research evidence for your answer.
    - What were the recommendations of the Canadian Development Report 1998 with regard to the corporate responsibility of Canadian companies doing business in developing countries?

2.  The following companies have been given recognition for their achievements in corporate social responsibility (as mentioned on the Conference Board of Canada site). Visit the web sites of each, discover why each company has been recognized in the area of corporate social responsibility and come prepared to class with your own list of the top three performers (complete with rationale):

    - Air Canada (http://www.aircanada.ca)
    - Alcan Aluminum Limited (http://www.alcan.com/)
    - CanWest Global (http://www.canwestglobal.com)
    - Canadian Imperial Bank of Commerce (http://www.cibc.com/index.html)
    - DuPont Canada (http://www.dupont.com/)
    - Herman Miller (http://www.hermanmiller.com/outline.html)
    - Imperial Oil (http://www.imperialoil.com/)
    - Noranda Inc. (http://www.noranda.com/ )
    - Syncrude Canada Ltd.(http:www.syncrude.com)
    - VanCity Savings Credit Union (http://www.vancity.com/)
    - One additional company of your choice (doing business in Canada today)

## PROCESS/INSTRUCTIONS:

1.  Your instructor will divide the class into small groups. Within your group, discuss the following topic: "Corporate Social Responsibility For Canadian Companies At home and In Developing Countries In The New Millenium". Summarize your discussion on a sheet of flip chart paper in bullet form and keep a careful record of your rationale.

2.     Your instructor will ask each group to outline the key points of its discussion (complete with rationale).

3.     Within your small group, share the information on the achievements in corporate social responsibility you discovered for the companies you researched on the Internet.

4.     Within your small group, each student will present his or her "Top Three Performers" list and give the supporting evidence from the web sites. The group will then attempt to reach consensus on the one top performer.

5.     Your instructor will ask each group in turn to present its top performer candidate (with complete rationale).

6.     Your instructor will ask the whole class to vote by secret ballot for the one final top performer. A volunteer from the class will be asked to count the ballots and announce the winner.


## DEBRIEFING:

1.     How important is corporate social responsibility in Canadian society today? What change, if any, do you foresee in the new millennium in this regard? Please explain your answer.

2.     Does corporate social responsibility have any effect on the bottom-line of companies doing business in Canada i.e., does "doing good" relate to "doing well"? Please explain your answer.

3. In what ways can a Canadian company demonstrate its good corporate citizenship in the developing countries in which it does business? Why will this essential in the coming years?

4. Do you agree with the class choice for the one top performing company? Please explain your answer.

5. What were the top five criteria used across the class in choosing the top performers? Did you use these same five criteria? Would you use these criteria if you were to start this exercise over again at this point? Please explain your answer.

**REFERENCES:**

1. Canadian Centre for Business in the Community (Conference Board of Canada), Taking Action on Corporate Social Responsibility: Trends in Corporate Social Responsibility; http://www2.conferenceboard.ca/ccbc/csroct98.htm

2. Canadian Centre for Business in the Community (Conference Board of Canada), Taking Action on Corporate Social Responsibility: Corporate Social Responsibility (CSR) Initiative; http://www2.conferenceboard.ca/ccbc/csrinit.htm

3. Ibid.

# 10. THERE'S NO BASE LIKE HOME:
## LOOKING AT THE PERSONAL SIDE OF TELECOMMUTING

 **LEARNING OBJECTIVES:**

1.   To stimulate individual research on the Internet on telecommuting/telework.

2.   To highlight the advantages and disadvantages of telecommuting for both the telecommuter worker and supervisor.

3.   To explore strategies for increasing the success of telecommuting programs.


## TYPE OF EXERCISE:

Individual activities and class-wide discussion


## RELATED CONCEPTS:

- Alternative work arrangements
- Telecommuting
- Work and home-life balance

 **TIME:** 40 minutes


The in-class time required to share a summary of the students' submissions will be 20 minutes. The reading of the second scenario and the debriefing will require another 20 minutes.


## BACKGROUND:

Traditionally, telecommuting has been initiated by employees with the main reason being to improve employee lifestyle. There is evidence of an increasing interest in telecommuting as a management practice.

A survey by consulting firm KPMG reported that of the 20% of the 2025 Canadian organizations who responded to their survey, 4.5% had telecommuters on staff and another 26% used telecommuters occasionally. This survey predicted that "the greatest increases [in telecommuting] are expected in professional, technical and middle management roles." In this survey, 91% of employers required that telecommuters be in the office on a regular or as needed basis and that the telecommuters stay in touch with the office between visits through the use of teleconferencing, e-mail and written documents.[1] It is clear telecommuting is here to stay. However, while it has its advantages, it is not always easy to juggle work and home life, especially when they are physically blended.

This exercise will help you to examine the advantages and challenges involved in telework.

 **MATERIALS NEEDED:**

- Two sheets of unlined legal-sized paper
- One sheet of lined letter-sized paper
- One sheet of unlined letter-sized paper

**PREASSIGNMENT STUDENT PREPARATION:**

1. Go to the Internet to research the telecommuting (also known as telework). The InnoVisions Canada's site at http://www.ivc.ca/ is an excellent place to start. On a sheet of lined letter-sized paper, make a list of all the sites you visit and note in point form three or four key features of each site. Print your name on the top of your website list.

2. Read the following scenario:

   *You are Aziz, a married twenty-nine year old father of two. Your wife, Erin, is a flight attendant with a Canadian airline company. You have a two year old son who attends play school three mornings week and a five year old daughter who is enrolled in full-day kindergarten. As a result of a motorcycle accident in your late teens, you have been confined to a wheelchair. Six months ago, your company, a non-unionized call centre with its headquarters located in the centre of large Canadian city offered you and your fellow call handlers the opportunity to participate in a year long telecommuting pilot program. Your supervisor explained that, while she was not altogether convinced that telecommuting was all it has been touted to be, she would allow her direct reports to take part in the pilot program. Further, she cautioned that they needed to be aware that the already stringent quotas would be increased and that she would be keeping very close tabs on their output.*

3.    Fold a sheet of unlined letter-sized paper in half from top to bottom. Turn the paper in "landscape" fashion. Entitle the left side "Aziz" and the right side "Supervisor". Answer the following questions in point form on a piece of paper. On the left side write your answer to the following question: Why do you think Aziz opted to participate in the telecommuting program in the first place? On the right side, answer the question: Why do you think his supervisor was so hesitant about the program at the beginning? Be sure to print your name on the top right of this paper.

4.    Fold a blank sheet of unlined legal-sized paper into three sections from top to bottom. Turn the paper sideways ("landscape" fashion) so that you have the three folds appearing from left to right. Write "Aziz - Six Months Into the Program" at the top of this sheet. On one third of the sheet, list all the advantages of telecommuting that Aziz would have realized from the program after the first six months. On the next third of the sheet, list all the disadvantages he would have noticed in this time. On the final third of the sheet, suggest strategies that could help Aziz to address the disadvantages. Be sure to include a list of all the human and material resources you would need to implement. Print your name on the top right of this sheet.

5.    Take a fresh sheet of unlined legal-sized paper. This time write "Supervisor - Six Months Into the Program" on the top of the sheet. Repeat Step 3. above but this time take the point of view of the supervisor.

6.    Hand in all four sheets to your instructor within the specified time frame. Be sure you have printed your name of each sheet.


## PROCESS/INSTRUCTIONS:

1.    In class, your instructor will display a summary of the websites and answers generated in Steps 1., 2., 3. and 4. of the PREASSIGNMENT STUDENT PREPARATION section.

2.    Read the follow-up scenario that will be distributed by your instructor.

**DEBRIEFING:**

1.     What are the current statistics on telework in Canada? How do you expect these statistics to change in the next five years?

2.     Which Canadian companies are using telework? At what levels are they using it?

3.     What are the advantages of telework for individual telecommuters? For companies? For the communities in which these companies are located?

4.     What are some of the possible disadvantages/challenges associated with telework for the individual teleworkers? For the supervisors?

5. How typical is the attitude of Aziz's supervisor? Why is she so skeptical about telecommuting? What training do supervisors require if their companies introduce telecommuting?

6. Discuss the conflicting feelings experienced by Aziz after six months.

7. What strategies and support mechanisms could be worked out between Aziz and his supervisor that would help him perform to the maximum in the telework program in the longer run?

## FOLLOW-UP ACTIVITIES:

1. Obtain from your instructor a copy of the master list of telework web sites displayed in class. Continue your research on the topic. Find out what the following terms mean: hoteling/free address and remote centres.

2. Contact one Canadian company which uses telework. Ask a company representative what type of personality best matches the challenges of telework.

3. Research other alternative work arrangements, such as: flexible hours, job sharing, sabbaticals, etc.

**REFERENCE:**

1.   Telecommuting Survey (1998); http://www.kpmg.ca/abc/vl/surveys/telcmut.htm

# 11. WITH THIS RING:
## ESTABLISHING THE CONTINGENCY EMPLOYMENT CONTRACT

 **LEARNING OBJECTIVES:**

1.  To understand the Canadian provincial and federal legal issues surrounding the employment contract.

2.  To identify the critical elements of an employment contact.

3.  To raise your awareness of the value of the employment contract.

## TYPE OF EXERCISE:

Individual Internet research, small group activities and class-wide discussion

## RELATED CONCEPTS:

- Legal issues in HR
- Federal and provincial employment law
- Employment contract
- Contingency workers

 **TIME:** 55 minutes

Small groups will typically require 5 minutes to brainstorm the benefits employers and employees reap from well-written employment contracts. The class presentation will take 10 minutes. The brainstorming of the elements of the employment contract is expected to take 5 minutes. Again, the class presentation will take 10 minutes. The sketching out of the contract for the consultant will require 15 minutes. The debriefing will take 10 minutes.

## BACKGROUND:

The number of contract workers (also called: contingency workers, temporary workers, non-staff workers, and flexible staff) has grown exponentially in Canada in recent years as a direct result of corporate downsizing, restructuring and globalization. Many employers have learned the hard way about the value of having a carefully written employment contract with contingency workers. Michael Failes, Vice President of Governmental Affairs, HRPAO and a lawyer sends a wake-up call to employers about the necessity of having written employment contracts: "Every employee is employed under a contract even if it is only a verbal contract. Without a formal written contract, the job offer becomes the contract."[1]

Doug Burn, in an article entitled: "Courts Set The Terms If You Don't", draws a comparison between employment contracts and prenuptial agreements. He points out that both types of agreements specify a number of important conditions, duties and responsibilities for the duration of the relationship. Burn adds: "But even the most elementary employment contract or pre-nuptial includes terms and conditions for ending the relationship." For Burn, these termination terms and conditions are a key reason for drawing up an employment contract. He cautions employers that the terms and conditions stated in the employment contract must comply with both federal and provincial employment standards.[2]

This exercise will give you an opportunity to understand the critical elements that must be written into an effective employment contract and to understand the legal issues involved in such a contract.

 **MATERIALS NEEDED:**

* Two sheets of flip chart paper and one marker for each small group
* One roll of masking tape

## PREASSIGNMENT STUDENT ASSIGNMENT:

Before the class in which you will completing this exercise, search the Internet for information on the following topics: employment contract (specifically, how to write an employment contract and elements of an employment contract) and federal and provincial labour standards (specifically, the Canada Labour Code, and employment standards for your province). You will find the following web sites to be very useful as a starting point for your search:

* http://labour-travail.hrdc-drhc.gc.ca/
* http://www.hroe.org
* http://www.minoritycareernet.com/newsltrs/96q4element.html
* http://smartbiz.com/sbs/arts/sbl2.htm

Be sure to bring the information you gather from this search to class.

## PROCESS/INSTRUCTIONS:

1. Your instructor will divide the class into small groups. Within your group, share the results of your Internet search on "the employment contract". Brainstorm the reasons why a well-written employment contract would be of benefit to: 1. an employer and 2. a contract worker. Record your lists on a sheet of flip chart paper.

2. Your instructor will invite each group to present its lists. As each group presents, the remaining groups will stroke off any item that has been mentioned by other groups to avoid duplication.

3. Within your small group, brainstorm the elements that must be included in an employment contract.

4. Each group will be invited to present its list of elements. As in the step above, the remaining groups will stroke off any item that has been mentioned.

5. Within your small group, pretend that you are members of the HR department of your school. You have decided to hire an independent human resource consultant to conduct some training over the next six months with your administrative supervisors. Using the yield from your brainstorming sessions today and your Internet research, sketch out an employment contract (words and phrases only under headings) for your newly hired consultant. Be sure that your contract does not in any way contravene either federal or provincial employment standards. Your instructor will allow only 15 minutes maximum in class and then will ask you to complete the contract in full form before the next class.

## DEBRIEFING:

1. Why should employers provide contract workers with a written contract? Why would contract workers want a written contract?

2. Why might an employer not want to have a written contract with a contract worker?

3. What are the key elements in a well-written employment contract?

4. What role do the federal and provincial employment standards play in employment contracts?

**REFERENCES:**

1. Burn, D. (1999, February/March). Courts set the Terms if you don't. *HR Professional*, p. 23.

2. Ibid., p. 25.

# PART 2

# BASIC HUMAN PROCESS

# 12. A MATCH TO LAST:
## A PERSONAL EXPLORATION OF
## THE PERSON-JOB FIT CONCEPT

 **LEARNING OBJECTIVES:**

1.      To sensitize you to the complexities of matching individuals and job requirements.

2.      To encourage you to reflect on the best work site match for your personality.

**TYPE OF EXERCISE:**

Individual Internet research and class-wide discussion

**RELATED CONCEPTS:**

*       Person-job fit
*       Personality

 **TIME:** 55 minutes

Individual students will take approximately 15 minutes to complete the OD-Online Personality Profiler, approximately 20 minutes to complete The Kiersey Temperament Sorter and another 10 minutes to review the job options associated with various personality types illustrated in the Self-Directed Search. The debriefing will require an additional 10 minutes.

**BACKGROUND:**

As you think about your class, or any other group of people you know well, you become aware of the wide variety of personality types among the members of the group. It is clear that some people are more temperamentally suited to certain occupations than others. While there is a vast body of literature, both historic and current, which examines the nature of personality,

51

practitioners in the area of organizational behaviour tend to focus on what has come to be known as the "Big Five" dimensions of personality. These include conscientiousness, extroversion-introversion, agreeableness, emotional stability, and openness to experience.[1]

The more you understand about your own personality, the better your ability to find a good job match. For example, you would expect that a job involving a lot of public speaking would be more uncomfortable for an introvert than for an extrovert. This exercise will give you the opportunity to explore your own personality type and to explore the best job match for you. Please note that this exercise does not constitute a formal assessment. The web sites suggested in this exercise provide little information about the scientific validity of the instruments they contain so results obtained from them should be treated accordingly.

## PREASSIGNMENT STUDENT PREPARATION:

1.  Visit the OD-Online Personality Profiler website (http://www17.web2010.com/od-online/webpage/profiler_chg.htm). This site will give you an overview of your personality profile based on the "big five" dimensions of personality.

2.  Next, visit The Kiersey Temperament Sorter (http://www.keirsey.com/cgi-bin/keirsey/newkts.cgi) which will give you feedback on your temperament type. Once you have received your feedback at the end of the questionnaire, you can explore the site to read about famous people whose temperaments are similar to yours. Their histories may give you some ideas about occupations to which you may be well suited. Click on "Keirsey Temperament Website" in the list at the bottom of the bar chart reporting your results. This will take you to the main menu. Click on "Temperament & Work". At the bottom of the description of the relationship between temperament and work, click on your temperament type to go to a page that describes the kinds of jobs for which you may be best suited.

3.  Finally, visit the Self-Directed Search site (http://www.sdstest2.com). While this site uses somewhat different personality descriptors from the previous sites, the concepts are related. Click on the labels (realistic, investigative, conventional, artistic, enterprising and social) to reveal information about the kinds of occupations that people who have each of these characteristics would find most appealing.

## PROCESS/INSTRUCTIONS:

In class, your instructor will lead a brief discussion about your experience in investigating the kinds of occupations that are suitable for people of different personality types.

**DEBRIEFING:**

1.    What aspects of this exercise did you find most surprising?

2.    Were the results you obtained from completing the questionnaires consistent with your view of yourself or do you think the questionnaires are invalid?

3.    How has this exercise impacted your thinking about your career options?

4.    What other dimensions of personality (beyond the Big-Five) do you think are useful for determining person-job fit?

5.       Discuss the usefulness of the "person-job fit" concept from the perspective of HR personnel who are primarily concerned with recruitment and selection.

6.       How does the "person-job fit" concept relate to work-related outcomes for individual job incumbents?

## FOLLOW-UP ACTIVITIES:

1.       Interview a person who is holding a job in which you have an interest. Discuss the personality characteristics this person feels are most important for his/her job.

2.       Guess who in your class has similar questionnaire results to the ones you obtained. Approach those people and, if they are willing, compare results. Notice whether you were right or wrong in your guesses. Discuss the occupations that interest people with similar questionnaire results.

## REFERENCE:

1.       Greenberg, J., Baron, R., Sales, C.A. and Owen, F.A. (2000). *Behaviour In Organizations*. Second Canadian Edition. Scarborough, Ontario: Prentice Hall Canada, pp. 104-105.

# 13. "BRAND YOU"[1]:
## CAREER DEVELOPMENT MEETS THE 21st CENTURY

 **LEARNING OBJECTIVES:**

1. To sensitize students to the impact of the "new" workforce on the career objectives and career path of new graduates.

2. To explore the "brand" concept as it relates to you as a future employee i.e., "Brand You".

3. To explore the potential impact of the "Brand You" concept on organizations.

**TYPE OF EXERCISE:**

Individual activities, small group activities and class-wide discussion

**RELATED CONCEPTS:**

- Career development
- HR and organizational trends analysis
- HR strategy development
- Reward and recognition

 **TIME:** 50 minutes

Small groups will typically require 20 minutes to critique the Peters' article and share Brand Equity Evaluation results. The drawing up of the positive and negative impacts lists and merging the results into master lists will require another 15 minutes. The debriefing session will require a minimum of 15 minutes.

## BACKGROUND:

In an article in *Fast Company* magazine (see web site: www.brandyou.com), Tom Peters makes the case for developing your image as a brand, "Brand You". Peters challenges employees to ask themselves a critical question, "What is it that my product or service does that makes it different?"[2] He recognizes that this question is a very tough one and that it requires demands a big adjustment in thinking. It requires that employees stop thinking of themselves as employees and start thinking of themselves as a brand. Peters advises them in his article: "You're not defined by your job title and you're not confined by your job description." He argues that they should set aside their job title as a description of what they do and, instead, implores them: "Ask yourself: What do I do that adds remarkable, measurable, distinguished and distinctive value?"[3]

From the perspective of HR professionals, the implications of Peters' thesis are considerable. The old days of a person's being hired by a company right out of college or university and then staying with that company for the rest of his or her working life are long gone. Instead, people entering the workforce in the 21st century can expect to have multiple careers and multiple organizational affiliations. To thrive in this competitive and fast-changing environment, each individual must be committed to continuous learning and self-promotion. Organizations that provide opportunities for multiple skill development tend to be more attractive than organizations that offer employees a traditional "job box" with limited access to new challenges.

 ## MATERIALS NEEDED:

- One copy of the article entitled: "The Brand Called You" by Tom Peters (August-September 1997). *Fast Company*. pp. 83-94 per student.

## PREASSIGNMENT STUDENT PREPARATION:

Locate and read the article: "The Brand Called You" by Tom Peters (as referenced above). Apply Peters' message to yourself by reflecting on the nature of our personal "brand" of knowledge, competencies, and personal qualities that could add value to a particular project or company. Complete Peters' Brand Equity Evaluation questionnaire which is printed as part of the article. Be sure to bring your copy of the article and your Brand Equity Evaluation results to class.

## PROCESS/INSTRUCTIONS:

1. Divide into small groups and ask each member to give his or her critique of the Peters' Brand You article and to share, on a voluntary basis, his or her results from the Brand Equity Evaluation. Determine if there is a general "buy-in" to the Brand You concept in your group. Your instructor will sit in with each group for a few minutes in order to learn the tenor of each group's discussion (and eventually the whole class).

2.    Your next task will be to discuss either the potential positive impacts OR the potential negative impacts on organizations if and when the majority of employees shift from loyalty to their company to loyalty to their own "brand". Your instructor will assign your group to the positive impacts side or the negative impacts side. Within the given time limit, brainstorm as many impacts as you can.

3.    All of the "positive" groups will join together to integrate and rationalize their lists into one master list. The "negative" groups will do the same. These master lists will then be photocopied for each member of the class. A short time (as specified by your instructor) will be set aside to ask for clarification or to challenge the information on the master lists.


## DEBRIEFING:

1.    In your opinion, will the "Brand You" concept really catch on in the work organizations of the 21st century or is it here now?

2.    Is it possible to have a strong sense of loyalty both to your organization and to yourself as an individual "brand"?

3.    Discuss the implications of an inter-generational conflict between baby boom managers and the so-called Generation X and Generation Y workers who are developing their own "brand" identity.

**FOLLOW-UP ACTIVITIES:**

1.  Search out Statistics Canada figures on the number of jobs the average Canadian can expect to have in an average 21st century career.

2.  Invite a career counselling professional to come to class to give his/her perspective on the Brand You concept and its likely impact of organizations in the 21st century and/or to make a presentation to the class on the basic skills needed for the job search process.

**REFERENCES:**

1.  Peters, T. (1997, August - September). The Brand Called You. *Fast Company*. pp. 83-94, quote p. 86.

2.  Ibid., p.86.

3.  Ibid.

# 14. SIT! STAY!:
## OPERANT CONDITIONING IN ACTION

 **LEARNING OBJECTIVES:**

1.     To demonstrate some of the principles of operant conditioning.

2.     To highlight the power of selective reinforcement in changing behaviour.

## TYPE OF EXERCISE:

Small group activities, role play and class-wide discussion

## RELATED CONCEPTS:

- Learning
- Selective reinforcement
- Organizational behaviour modification
- Shaping
- Non-verbal communication

 **TIME:** 35 minutes

Small groups will be given 5 minutes to review their notes and 10 minutes to conduct the interview. The observer reports will require 10 minutes. The debriefing will require an additional 10 minutes.

 **MATERIALS NEEDED:**

- One copy of either the interviewer role instruction sheet, the interviewee role instruction sheet or the observer role instruction sheet for each student in the class - each role sheet printed on a different coloured sheet (to be distributed by your instructor).

59

## PROCESS/INSTRUCTIONS:

1.     Your instructor will designate one third of the class as "interviewers", one third as "interviewees", and one third as "observers" by randomly distributing three different role instruction sheets which have been colour-coded. Do not share your role instruction information with anyone else.

2.     Join with two other class members who have a differently coloured role sheet (compared to yours and to each other) i.e., your new group of three will consist of an interviewer, an interviewee and an observer. Read and think about your role instructions in silence for 5 minutes.

3.     The interviewer and interviewee will be seated facing one another at a distance of no more than one metre. The observer will sit no more than one metre away from the interviewer and interviewee and will sit so as to be able to see the faces of both the interviewer and the interviewee at all times.

4.     The interviewer will conduct a ten minute interview with the interviewee while the observer watches in silence and makes notes on the process.

5.     Your instructor will ask the observers in turn to give a brief report.

## DEBRIEFING:

1.     What principles of operant conditioning were demonstrated during the interviews?

2.     What was the major technique used by the interviewer?

3. How does an animal trainer teach a dog to sit? Compare the animal trainer's techniques with those used by the interviewer in the role play in class today.

**FOLLOW-UP ACTIVITIES:**

1. Visit a dog training school and ask about the use of learning techniques.

2. Invite a psychologist to class to discuss the use of selective reinforcement and behaviour modification techniques.

## 15.  THE WHOLE TRUTH AND NOTHING BUT THE TRUTH: USING 360 - DEGREE FEEDBACK TO IMPROVE TEAM PERFORMANCE

 **LEARNING OBJECTIVES:**

1.    To highlight the potential benefits and pitfalls of using 360-degree performance feedback systems.

2.    To learn about the various applications of 360 systems.

3.    To learn about design strategies for avoiding the potential pitfalls of 360 systems.

**TYPE OF EXERCISE:**

Individual Internet research, small group discussion and class-wide discussion

**RELATED CONCEPTS:**

- Performance management
- HR development
- Team performance
- Perception
- Coaching
- Leadership and supervision

 **TIME:** 55 minutes

Small groups will typically require 15 minutes to answer the questions on the 360 method of performance feedback. The crafting of the statements and the presentation to the class will take 10 minutes and 15 minutes respectively. The reaction to the instructor's announcement will require 5 minutes. The debriefing will require an additional 10 minutes.

## BACKGROUND:

Along with, and perhaps in some ways because of, the dramatic increase in the use of teams in work organizations, there has been a "surge of interest" in a performance assessment tool known as 360-degree feedback or multi-source/multi-level feedback. For example, in 1997, one writer pegged the usage of 360 systems in U.S. organizations at 8 percent but added that 69 percent planned to introduce it in the next three years.[1] Another author more recently estimated that in the U.S. more than 90 percent of the major companies are using some form of multi-source assessment.[2]

> The 360-degree performance feedback system is designed to provide feedback to an employee from various individuals who regularly interact with that individual in the course of his/her job such as team members, supervisor, customers, etc. Of all its various applications such as employee development, HR decision tool for promotion, termination or compensation, management and leadership development, perhaps the most effective is employee development. Provided of course that the system has been well planned, designed and implemented.[3]

This exercise will give you the opportunity to explore in depth the multi-source assessment system of performance management.

## PREASSIGNMENT STUDENT PREPARATION:

Before the class in which you will be completing this exercise, research 360-degree feedback performance systems on the Internet. You should explore the following topics/materials (at minimum):

- I. Debare's article on 360 reprinted from the *San Francisco Chronicle* at: http://www.sfgate.com/cgi-bin/article.cgi?file=/chronicle/archive/1997/05/05/BU65200.DTL

- R. Nagel's article on 360 at: http://www.ipma-hr.org/global/360au.html

- Con-way Transportation Services' first hand account of its own 360 system called "The Team Improvement Review" at: http://www.fastcompany.com/online/17/conway.html

- Links to Performance Measurement-Related Topics at: http://www.zigonperf.com/Links.htm

 **MATERIALS NEEDED:**

- Two sheets of flip chart paper and one marker for each small group
- One roll of masking tape

**PROCESS/INSTRUCTIONS:**

1. Your instructor will divide the class into five small groups. Within your group, review the results of your Internet research by answering the following questions:

   What does a "typical" 360-degree system look like i.e., Who provides the performance feedback?, How many people provide input?, Does the rated individual know who gave what feedback?, What criteria are rated?, How are the results tabulated?, How is the supervisor involved in the performance system?

   What are the potential benefits for work organizations and for individual employees of using 360-degree feedback?

   What are the potential pitfalls of a 360 system?

   Describe Con-Way's TIR system. How does it capitalize on the benefits of the 360 system and yet avoid the pitfalls?

   What are the keys to a successful 360 system?

2. Your instructor will assign two of the following dimensions of team performance to each group:

   - commitment to excellence,
   - flexibility,
   - balance between task-orientation and relationship orientation,
   - trust,
   - participation and involvement,
   - support to team members,
   - quality of performance,
   - willingness to confront and resolve conflict,
   - candid and open discussion,
   - receptivity to members' ideas

3.	Within your group, craft three statements for each of your assigned team dimensions to be used as part of a 360 questionnaire/instrument. For example, if your dimension is "commitment to excellence," one statement could read: "This individual can be depended upon to deliver quality contributions." The following scale would then be used to evaluate a team member on this dimension:

Never       Rarely       Sometimes       Often       Always
   1 ---------- 2 ---------- 3 ---------- 4 ---------- 5

4.	Your instructor will ask each group in turn to present its statements. After each group presents, the class as a whole will be given a chance to suggest any improvements on each statement.

5.	Pretend that your small group is actually the group with whom you are working currently on group project for this course (or any other course you are taking). Your instructor will give you some additional information at this point. Discuss your reaction to his/her announcement. Translate the announcement into the language of a team in a work organization. What lesson can be learned from this about 360 systems and their applications?

## DEBRIEFING:

1.	As an employee who works as part of a team, how would you welcome your company's decision to change from an annual one-on-one appraisal system with your supervisor to a 360-degree assessment? Please explain your answer.

2.	What are the best applications for the 360 system?

3.      What are the most controversial applications for the 360 system?

4.      If you were a supervisor responsible for overseeing the performance of a team, would you welcome your company's decision to change to a 360 system? Please explain your answer.

5.      Should your instructor adapt some of the methodologies of the 360 system into his/her evaluation of group projects? Please explain your answer.

6.      What are the keys to an effective 360 system?

**REFERENCES:**

1.	Debare, I. 360-Degrees of Evaluation: More Companies Turning To Full-Circle Job Reviews; http://www.sfgate.com/cgi-bin/article.cgi?file=/chronicle/archive/1997/05/05/BU65200.DTL

2.	Nagel, R. The 360-Degree Feedback Avalanche; http://www.ipma-hr.org/global/360au.html

3.	Ibid.

# 16. YOU'RE LUCKY I'M SO OBJECTIVE:
## SELECTION DECISIONS AND OBJECTIVITY

 **LEARNING OBJECTIVES:**

1.    To give you an opportunity to examine the objectivity of selection decisions.

2.    To make you aware of "opportunities" for perceptual biases during the selection process.

## TYPE OF EXERCISE:

Individual activity, small group activities and class-wide discussion

## RELATED CONCEPTS:

- Recruitment and selection
- Perception
- Individual differences

 **TIME:** 40 minutes

The individual ranking activity will typically take 5 minutes. The first small group activity in which students reach a consensus ranking will require 15 minutes. Finally, the second group activity and debriefing will take 10 minutes each.

## BACKGROUND:

Matching an individual applicant with the right job is a complex and, most often, subjective process. Selection is a core function for HR professionals. A lot rests on finding the right talent to add value to an organization and mistakes can be costly. Hiring mistakes can lead to wrongful dismissal lawsuits that can be expensive both financially and in terms of poor public relations both inside and outside of the organization. This puts considerable pressure on the HR professional who must insure that the match of person and job is as good as possible.

68

 **MATERIALS NEEDED:**

- One applicant profile and one rating sheet for each student in the class (to be distributed by your instructor)
- One transparency marker and two rating sheets copied onto transparency sheets for each group
- One transparency marker and rating sheets copied onto transparency sheets for the student who tallies the votes
- One applicant profile for each student in the class (to be distributed by the instructor)


**PROCESS/INSTRUCTIONS:**

1.  Please read the following scenario:

    *You are a Human Resource professional employed by a large marketing company in downtown Fredericton, New Brunswick. Your company is growing rapidly and is expanding globally. Your job is to select staff for a large number of entry level positions for the company's branch offices in Fredericton and the immediate surrounding area. You have finished all the interviews with the applicants for all positions and have now reached the final stage in the selection decision process. Today you are making the final decision on the applicants for the telemarketing positions. In fact, you have only one more applicant for whom you will make a final "accept/reject" decision before you leave for the day.*

2.  Your instructor will ask for one volunteer from the class who will tally the rating sheets as soon as they are handed in at the end of this step. Next, your instructor will distribute a short applicant profile and a rating scale to each person in the class. Please do not discuss the applicant or rating scale with anyone else. As soon as you receive the profile, read it thoroughly, complete the rating scale and write your identification number (found on the top right of your copy of the profile). Your instructor will collect the completed rating scales. You will keep the applicant profile with you.

3.  Divide into small groups according to the FIRST number of your identification number i.e., all number 1s (11, 12, 13, 14, etc.) will form a group, all the 2s (21, 22, 23, 24, 25) will form a group and so on until all students are in a group. Your instructor will assist you by calling out one number at a time and indicating where your group will work.

4.  Your job is to reach a consensus (on all three questions on the rating sheet and the accept/reject final decision). When your group has reached a consensus, obtain from your instructor a transparency sheet which has a copy of the rating sheet printed on it. <u>Mark the number of your group as your identification number on the top of the sheet</u> i.e., a 1 or 2 or 3, etc. and then complete the sheet indicating the group's position on the applicant. Hand the completed transparency sheet to the instructor.

5.  Divide into a different small group. This time divide on the basis of your SECOND number of your identification number i.e., all the "1s" form a group (11, 21, 31, 41, 51, etc.), all the 2s form a group (12, 22, 32, 42, etc.) until all students are in a new group. Repeat Step 4. above. This time your group number will be the second number that you all have in common. The tally sheet will bear this number and the words "Mixed Group" written on the top.

6.  The student who tallied the results of the first vote now share the results with the class. The instructor will share the rest of the results.


## DEBRIEFING

1.  Compare and contrast the individual votes with those of the groups.

2.  Were the results of the second vote on the applicant rating sheet very different from your own individual ranking on your first rating sheet? How do you explain the results now?

3.  What was the real purpose of this exercise? Did it succeed in its purpose?

## 17.  WOW! LOOK AT ME I'M A TRAINER: TEACHING CLASSMATES A SKILL

 **LEARNING OBJECTIVES:**

1.      To provide an opportunity for students to test their own theories on how people learn.

2.      To introduce HR students to steps in the On-the-Job-Training process.

## TYPE OF EXERCISE:

Brief skill lessons taught by students randomly selected from the class and class wide discussion.

## RELATED CONCEPTS:

- Operant conditioning
- Contingencies of reinforcement
- On-The-Job Training (OJT)

 **TIME:** 75 minutes

Your instructor will require 5 minutes to train the observers.  Five students will be given 10 minutes each to conduct the skill lessons (minimum of five lessons = 50 minutes total).  The reports from the observers will require a total of 10 minutes.  The debriefing will take an additional 10 minutes.

## BACKGROUND:

This exercise introduces you to the realities of the world of the trainer. This exercise will help you to grapple with the practical challenges faced by trainers and will give you an experiential context for the course material on learning/training in an organization.

 **MATERIALS NEEDED:**

- One 3" by 5" lined index card for each student
- Six "Observer Sheets" for the six individuals chosen, for this task (supplied by your instructor)
- One copy of "THE FOUR STEP METHOD OF ON-THE-JOB TRAINING: GUIDELINES" for each student

## PREASSIGNMENT STUDENT PREPARATION:

Please come to class prepared to teach the class a brief skill lesson (i.e., how to tie a man's tie, how to do a certain dance, how to do a card trick, how to fold a paper airplane, etc. (Props are allowed.)

## PROCESS/INSTRUCTIONS:

1. Your instructor will ask you to print (on an index card) your name and the name of the lesson you are prepared to teach the class. Your instructor will then collect the completed index cards and shuffle them in your presence.

2. Your instructor will then ask for six students to volunteer to be observers (i.e., these students will not be teaching a skill lesson but will, rather, observe each lesson and complete a structured observation sheet under the direction of your instructor.

3. Your instructor will ask for five volunteer "trainers". If five students don't volunteer, your instructor will then ask a student to choose at random the required number of index cards from the collected set.

4. Your instructor will give the class a 5 minute break while he/she trains the observers for their task.

5. The five trainers will each be given 10 minutes to conduct their training sessions. If a trainer has not finished his/her lesson in the 10 minute period, your instructor will interrupt and ask the trainer to outline what he/she had planned to do from that point on. The five training sessions will run back-to-back without comment from the instructor or the observers.

6. After the training sessions have been completed, trainers will be given a chance to "vent" their feelings. After this, the class members (other than the trainers and the observers) will be given a chance to express their opinions of the training sessions. Your instructor will then explain the task of the observers and will begin to reveal the true purpose of the

exercise. Next, the observers will give their reports one after the other. Your instructor will make some final observations on the training sessions and will hand to each student a copy of: "THE FOUR STEP METHOD of ON-THE-JOB TRAINING: GUIDELINES".

7.      Your instructor will pass around the complete set of index cards to abate curiosity on what the class missed by not hearing all the lessons.


**DEBRIEFING:**

1.      What were the prevailing assumptions by the trainers about how people learn?

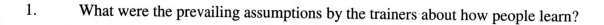

2.      Reconcile these assumptions with learning theories and OJT methodology.

3.      Did the "learners" really learn? What evidence do you have to support your answer?

4.    How would the class members (not the trainers and not the observers) improve on the training they received?

5.    If you were a trainer during this exercise, how do you feel about your experience now that it is over?  Do you think you would make a good trainer? Please explain your answer.

**FOLLOW-UP ACTIVITIES:**

Discuss the old adages:

    1.    "If the learner didn't learn, the teacher didn't teach."

    2.    "You can't teach an old dog new tricks."

## 18. BAD MEMORIES COME FLOODING BACK: DESIGNING A LEARNING SPACE FOR ADULT LEARNERS

 **LEARNING OBJECTIVES:**

1.  To increase your awareness of the messages communicated to participants by the physical set-up of the learning space.

2.  To give you the opportunity to apply the principles of adult learning in the design of a learning space for a management development program.

**TYPE OF EXERCISE:**

Individual activities, role play and small group activities

**RELATED CONCEPTS:**

- HR development
- Principles of adult learning
- Pedagogy and andragogy
- Design of physical space for adult learning

 **TIME:** 45 minutes

Individual activities will typically require 15 minutes. Small group activities will take 15 minutes. The instructor wrap-up and debriefing will require an additional 15 minutes.

**BACKGROUND:**

The physical design of a learning space sets the tone for any training session. For example, participants who enter a training room filled with chairs in straight rows immediately will get the message that they will be listening to the person at the front of the room and not interacting with and learning from their peers throughout the session. For some participants, such as the supervisor (Jack) whom you will get to know quite well during this exercise, this may trigger some bad memories from their long-past school days. A trainer who pays scant attention to the design of the learning space is missing out on a vital learning tool.

A key to understanding the important, if "silent", contribution made by the physical layout of the learning space to effective adult education can be found in the considerable works of Malcolm Knowles on "the art and science of helping adults learn" (andragogy).[1] Knowles was keenly aware that adults do learn differently from children. According to his writing, adult learners as compared with children tend to be self-directing, have accumulated more experience, have a different readiness to learn and are problem-centered.

This exercise will teach you how to apply the principles of andragogy (as opposed to pedagogy) to the physical design of a learning space for adult learners.

 **MATERIALS NEEDED:**

- Three blank sheets of paper and one pencil with a large eraser for each small group (to be distributed by your instructor)
- One overhead transparency sheet and one marker per group

**PROCESS/INSTRUCTIONS:**

1. Please read the scenario below.

   *Jack is a 47 year old supervisor in a large well-known, manufacturing plant. He quit school on the very day he reached the legal age. This was the birthday present he had dreamed about since he first began having trouble with his reading in grade two when he watched his classmates "getting gold stars" (as he called it) for their writing and oral reading assignments. By the time he quit, he was able to read only at about a grade four level, just enough to just get by. The humiliation of years of poor report cards had taken its toll. He promised himself from an early age that he would take charge of his own life as soon as he could. The day he quit school he wiped his feet on the school doormat as he was leaving, as if to wipe off the dust of hurt and shame of his unhappy school years.*

   *Despite his academic shortcomings, Jack had many other strengths which he put to good use from the time he was hired in the unionized manufacturing plant. His commitment to hard work and his ability to find innovative solutions to mechanical problems quickly got the attention of production management. First he was made lead hand and then later he was promoted to supervisor. He has been a supervisor for the last twenty years. His performance reviews have been outstanding over the years and his work group likes and respects him tremendously.*

*While Jack is very happy overall in his job, he does have some heavy personal concerns right now. His wife of 28 years, Donna, is recovering more slowly than expected from a stroke she suffered last year. To make matters worse, just last month, Jack lost a large amount of money in mutual funds and is having trouble meeting the mortgage payments on his aging house.*

*Today at the plant when he checked his e-mail he discovered that, in less than three weeks, he and 39 other supervisors at the plant must attend a management development program. The title of the training series is: Principles of Supervision in A Heavy Manufacturing Plant. The sessions are to be held in the conference room of the old hotel down the street from the plant. There will be five 3-hour sessions which will start immediately at the end of Jack's shift (4:00 pm for each of the five sessions). The announcement further indicated that all the supervisors are to complete "substantial" reading assignments before each session. Jack called up his long time buddy, Bill who is also a supervisor at the plant. If anyone knew more about this, it would be Bill.*

*According to Bill, the sessions would be taught by a professor who had never been a supervisor - much less seen the inside of a plant like theirs. Rumours were flying too that the production manager would be there for each session, that there would be a two-hour exam at the end of the sessions and that the supervisors who failed the test would lose their jobs! No one can figure out why on earth management would choose to start these sessions in just over two weeks when production in the plant is at an all time high.*

2.  Each and every student in the room will now "step into Jack's shoes". In a few minutes, your instructor will ask you to leave the room for five minutes. When you return you will be Jack who is just entering the hotel conference room on the first day of the Management Development series. Take a good look around, Jack, since no one else seems to be here yet.

3.  Your instructor will ask you take out a couple of blank sheets of paper and a pencil. On these pieces of paper, you will jot down your answers to two questions which your instructor will pose in a few minutes. You may write your answers in point form. No one but the instructor will speak until both questions have been asked and answered (in writing). Your instructor will now ask the two questions.

4.  Your instructor will choose two volunteers (one for each question) to go to the chalkboard and write while the rest of you share your answers to each question in turn in round-robin fashion.

5.  Your instructor will divide the class into five-person groups. Your task will be to design a learning space which would be most appropriate for 20 supervisors (we'll assume for the sake of this exercise that the supervisors are very similar to Jack) and which would

work in a reasonably-sized hotel conference room. Your design will take the form of a labeled floor plan which shows the placement of tables, chairs, A/V equipment, etc. Be sure to appoint a recorder for your group. Ask the recorder to obtain three sheets of blank paper from your instructor (cut in the shape of the conference room), a pencil with an eraser, one blank transparency sheet and one transparency marker. Try out a few designs on the pieces of paper before you choose your final plan. Have your recorder draw this final plan on the transparency sheet.

6.      Each recorder in turn will explain her or his group's plan and will show how the plan would answer Jack's concerns and would facilitate his learning.


**DEBRIEFING:**

1.      How can the physical set-up of a learning space enhance the learning experience for adults? Please explain your answer.

2.      How can the physical set-up of a learning space detract from the learning? Please explain your answer.

3.      How can a trainer translate the principles of adult learning into an effective and pleasant learning space design?

**FOLLOW-UP ACTIVITIES:**

1.      Invite to your class a  professional trainer from an industrial setting similar to Jack's as soon as possible. Ask the trainer in what ways he/she feels that adult learners such as Jack are different from learners who are children. Ask the trainer to describe his/her preferred room set-up for the delivery of management development programs (similar to the one Jack is anticipating).

2.      Visit one or more professional training facilities out in your community e.g., such as one operated by a bank or trust company. Note your feelings upon entering the room and the physical set-up including furnishings and placement of equipment. Ask about the various kinds of training activities are conducted in that room.


**REFERENCE:**

1.      Knowles, M. (1972, November). The Manager As An Educator. *Journal of Continuing Education and Training*, Vol. 2 (2), 97-105.

## 19. A NEW KIND OF SMART:
## THE RISE OF EMOTIONAL INTELLIGENCE

 **LEARNING OBJECTIVES:**

1.    To increase your awareness of the concept of emotional intelligence.

2.    To give you an opportunity to discover your own Emotional Quotient (EQ).

## TYPE OF EXERCISE:

Individual Internet exercise, small group activities and class-wide discussion

## RELATED CONCEPTS:

- Emotional intelligence (EQ)
- Individual differences
- Career development
- Learning
- HR development
- Motivation
- Recruitment and selection

 **TIME:** 35 minutes

The small groups will typically require 15 minutes to discuss the results of their Internet search on emotional intelligence and to identify behavioural interview questions. The class presentations of the interview questions will take 10 minutes. An additional 10 minutes will be required for debriefing.

## BACKGROUND:

Daniel Goleman's work in the area of Emotional Intelligence (EQ) has become popular in a wide variety of circles from popular culture to education to business. Goleman defines high EQ "as self-awareness, self-regulation, motivation, empathy and social skills... ." In his survey of 121 organizations Goleman found that "two out of every three abilities listed were in the emotional realm"[1]

The application of EQ to leadership in business is based on four cornerstones: emotional literacy, emotional fitness, emotional depth and emotional alchemy. Emotional literacy refers to areas such as emotional energy, honesty and intuition. Emotional fitness includes resilience, renewal and authentic presence. Emotional depth involves accountability, commitment and conscience, among other factors. Emotional alchemy includes the development of intuitive flow that contributes to creative problem solving.[2] Some of the key skills related to these factors include self-awareness, self-control, motivation, empathy and social skills.[3] These emotional skills are becoming increasingly important in organizations learning to live with rapid change.[4]

This exercise will give you the opportunity to assess your own EQ and to consider how you can probe for EQ factors during the selection process.

 ## MATERIALS NEEDED:

- One sheet of flip chart paper and one marker for each small group
- One roll of masking tape

## PREASSIGNMENT STUDENT PREPARATION:

Before the class in which you will be completing this exercise, visit the Utne Reader site at http://www.utne.com/cgi-bin/eq  Here you will find a page entitled: "What's Your Emotional Intelligence Quotient? You'll Find Out Soon...." by Daniel Goleman. Answer the questions on the page and then press the "What's My Quotient" button. This will take you to a page that will give you your EQ score on the questionnaire. This site also includes a detailed explanation of the scoring. Reflect on your score. Are you surprised by your results? Were you aware of your level of emotional intelligence before this exercise?

## PROCESS/INSTRUCTIONS:

1.    Your instructor will divide the class into discussion groups of three people. In your group, discuss Goleman's process/questionnaire for assessing your emotional intelligence. Did you agree or disagree with your own EQ score? What other questions would you suggest as measures of emotional intelligence? Are there other suggestions you would have for Goleman about assessing emotional intelligence?

2.  Your instructor will ask volunteers to share the essence of the group discussions from Step 1. above.

3.  With your group members discuss the implications of the concept of emotional intelligence for work organizations for the recruitment and selection process. Conclude your discussion by writing five behavioural description interview questions which would tap Goleman's concept and model of emotional intelligence. (Behavioural description questions are those which prompt an applicant to describe what he or she did in a situation in the past. Such questions may be prefaced with: "Please tell me about a time when you gave negative feedback to one of your direct reports.") Record your questions on a sheet of flip chart paper.

4.  Your instructor will ask each group in turn to present its behavioural interview questions to the class.


## DEBRIEFING:

1.  Reflect on a difficult working relationship you have experienced at work or in a student project group. Consider how the concept of emotional intelligence may be useful in understanding the difficulties you experienced.

2.  Reflect on what you have learned about yourself by doing this exercise. What areas of your own emotional intelligence would you like to develop? How do you plan to develop these areas?

3.    Is it possible to increase a person's emotional intelligence? If you answered "yes", what educational programs could organizations put in place which would increase the EQ of organizational members?

**REFERENCES:**

1.    Walmsley, A. (1998, November 21). EQ in the office. *The Globe and Mail*, p. D15.

2.    Cooper, R.K. and Sawaf, A. (1997). *Executive EQ: Emotional Intelligence in Leadership and Organizations.* New York: Advanced Intelligence Technologies, LLC.

3.    Staff Writer (1998, November 21). Beyond expertise: a different kind of smart. *The Globe and Mail,* p. D15.

4.    Walmsley, A., ibid.

# PART 3

# THE INDIVIDUAL IN THE ORGANIZATION

# 20. BEYOND CARROTS AND STICKS:
## APPLYING MOTIVATION MODELS

 **LEARNING OBJECTIVES:**

1.      To give you the opportunity to apply a number of motivation theories.

2.      To give you the opportunity to gain a deeper understanding of a variety of motivation concepts and theories.

## TYPE OF EXERCISE:

Individual activities, small group activities and class-wide discussion

## RELATED CONCEPTS:

•       Application of motivation concepts and theories

 **TIME:** 45 minutes

Small groups will typically require 20 minutes to read the five scenarios and to understand "what's going on" with the assistance of one or more of the five motivation models. The group presentations of the scenarios will take 15 minutes. The debriefing will require an additional 10 minutes.

## BACKGROUND:

Motivation is one of the most important issues facing workers and managers alike. Whether an organization emphasizes team work or individual contributions to the organization's functioning, the key to success is helping people to be motivated to produce their best work. Understanding motivation can be challenging. Many theorists have tackled this complex subject. This exercise will give you experience applying motivation models.

## PREASSIGNMENT STUDENT PREPARATION:

Before the class in which you will be completing this exercise review the following motivation theories in your organizational behaviour textbook:

- Alderfer's ERG Theory
- Locke and Latham's Goal-Setting Theory
- Adams' Equity Theory
- Porter and Lawler's Expectancy Theory
- Hackman and Oldham's Job Characteristics Model

Please bring your textbook to class.

## PROCESS/INSTRUCTIONS:

1. Your instructor will divide the class into small groups.

2. Please read the following scenarios. Within your small group, decide which of the following motivation models is (or are) the most useful as you discuss "what's going on" in each scenario:

- Alderfer's ERG Theory
- Locke and Latham's Goal-Setting Theory
- Adams' Equity Theory
- Porter and Lawler's Expectancy Theory
- Hackman and Oldham's Job Characteristics Model

---

## SCENARIO 1:

*You are an accounting major in a Canadian post-secondary institution. You are currently taking an introductory Organizational Behaviour course. So far in your post-secondary education, you have encountered little difficulty with getting straight As in your courses, especially in your accounting courses. Your OB course, however, is turning into a nightmare for you. You managed to get 53 per cent on your OB midterm, one of the lowest marks in the class. Your classmates in the OB course, you discover, are mainly social science majors e.g., majors in psychology and sociology, and they are getting As and Bs. You have never taken a psychology or sociology course - even though there is a social science prerequisite for this OB course. You applied and received an override into the course because of your several co-op work term experiences. Further, the comments written on your midterm by your instructor seem to indicate that you are either "way off the mark" with your answers or that you are not explaining your answers in enough depth. You are desperate to raise your grade to at least a high B by the end of the course. You decide to go to talk with your instructor.*

---

**SCENARIO 2:**

*You are a sign painter employed by a small local business in your home town. You pride yourself on your creativity and accuracy. It has always been important to you to keep learning in your job, especially about new techniques and materials. You are very interested in learning how to run your own sign painting business. While you enjoy the many opportunities you have to work alone on projects, you sometimes wish you could have direct contact with the customers who order the signs you paint. Your supervisor, with whom you rarely talk, called you into her office yesterday and informed you that over the past three months several customers have complained about errors on the signs you painted. You were instantly upset and confused by this unexpected news. You do recall several occasions when you could not read the written order forms completed by the customer service reps on the front desk. You have decided to cool down for a few days and then go to talk with your supervisor.*

---

**SCENARIO 3:**

*You are a student in an introductory Organizational Behaviour class in a post-secondary institution. You learn that your classmate received 9 marks out of 10 on the one question you were sure you had "aced" on the midterm exam. Your mark on this question turned out to be a 7. In a further conversation with your classmate you discover that his mark on the question was originally a 7 but, when he complained about the mark, the instructor reread his answer and decided to raise it to a 9. Your classmate was so delighted with the raised mark that he insisted that you read his answer to the question. After reading his answer, you smile and politely say "congratulations". You decide to go to your instructor and ask for your answer to be reread.*

---

**SCENARIO 4:**

*You are an assembly-line worker in a large non-unionized manufacturing company. Your work team has just been informed that its production targets have been raised by 10% without any input from the members of the workforce. You had a quota increase six months ago that you and your colleagues feel has pushed you to the limit of your capacity to produce products within the minimum allowable quality parameters. You believe that if you increase your production rate your accuracy rate will drop and you will be penalized for producing poor quality goods. Management has not talked with you about the reasons for the increase at this time. In fact, the workers in your company do not know what direction the company is pursuing. Management keeps telling you to produce more goods at a faster rate but you have no idea where it will all end. You and you colleagues start picturing yourselves like Lucille Ball trying to keep up with the increased line rate in the chocolate factory only you know that, unlike Lucy, you cannot eat your mistakes!*

---

## SCENARIO 5:

*For the past two years you have been enjoying your creative and challenging job in a small but rapidly growing Canadian high tech company. You have been extremely pleased with the collegial and supportive working environment since your first day. Constantly over your two year tenure with this company, you have been recognized by your supervisor for your work accomplishments. You have often wished that you were more highly paid but you recognize that this is a rapidly growing small business with resources already stretched to the hilt. Suddenly, your world has been turned upside-down. Your widowed mother back home has been diagnosed with a life-threatening illness and now has turned to you for financial and emotional support. You realize that you must consider taking a high paying manual labour job in a large company in your home town to fulfill your family responsibilities.*

---

3.    Your instructor will ask each group in turn to give its understanding of a different scenario and to explain how the motivation theories assisted the group in its task.

**DEBRIEFING:**

1.     Think about a time when you were very frustrated at home, at work or at school. As you reflect on this, which motivation model is most helpful to you in analyzing the situation?

2.     As you reviewed the five motivation models in preparation for this exercise, what similarities and differences did you notice among them? What do you think is missing in these theories?

3.     Speculate on how two or more of these theories could be integrated to form a "super theory" of motivation.

**FOLLOW-UP ACTIVITIES:**

1.     Work with your small group colleagues to write a scenario that illustrates your "favourite" motivation theory. Imagine that you are writing this scenario to explain this theory to a manager who does not have prior knowledge of the motivation model.

2.     Pick a union-management dispute story from a newspaper or magazine. Use the theories of motivation that were the focus of this exercise to analyze the motivational issues underlying the dispute.

# 21. I'D RATHER DO IT MYSELF:
## A MOTIVATION MODEL-BUILDING WORKSHOP

 **LEARNING OBJECTIVES:**

1.      To facilitate your review of a number of work motivation models.

2.      To give you the opportunity to build your own model of motivation.

3.      To encourage you to think about the possibilities of synthesizing and integrating various concepts from a variety of well-respected and researched models of motivation.

**TYPE OF EXERCISE:**

Individual activities, small group activities and class-wide discussion

**RELATED CONCEPTS:**

*       Models of motivation
*       Research methodology
*       Independent variables
*       Dependent variables
*       Intervening variables
*       Moderator variables

 **TIME**: 75 minutes

Small groups will be given a time limit of 10 minutes to discuss the criteria for a good theory/good motivation theory. The class-wide discussion on these criteria and the definitions of the four types of variables will take 10 minutes. The model-building and research planning activities in the small groups will require 20 minutes. Group presentations of the new models of motivation will take 20 minutes. The debriefing will require an additional 15 minutes.

## PREASSIGNMENT STUDENT PREPARATION:

1. Before the class in which you will be completing this exercise, review the following five motivation theories in your organizational behaviour textbook:

   - Alderfer's ERG Theory
   - Locke and Latham's Goal-setting Theory
   - Adams' Equity Theory
   - Porter and Lawler's Expectancy Theory
   - Hackman and Oldham's Job Characteristics Model

   Please bring your text to class.

2. Define and distinguish each of the following types of research variables: independent, dependent, intervening and moderator. Which of the motivation models listed in Step 1. above feature(s) all of these four types of variables? Why is this noteworthy? Please bring your notes to class.

 **MATERIALS NEEDED:**

- One dark-coloured large sheet of medium-weight cardboard for each small group
- Two 2 inch square pads of sticky notes (one yellow pad and one blue pad) for each small group
- One marker for each small group
- One roll of masking tape

## PROCESS/INSTRUCTIONS:

1. Your instructor will divide the class into small groups.

2. Within your small group discuss the following questions: What is a good theory? What is a good motivation theory? The time limit for this discussion is 10 minutes.

3. First, your instructor will ask each group in round-robin fashion to suggest one criterion of a "good theory". A volunteer will be chosen from the class to act as the chalkboard recorder. Secondly, after all criteria have been suggested and the class has reached consensus on the list, the instructor will repeat the process with the second question i.e., What is a good motivation theory? Again the key points will be written on the chalkboard and a consensus reached on the final list. Thirdly, your instructor will ask for volunteers to share their definitions of the four types of variables i.e., independent, dependent, intervening and moderator. Fourthly, your instructor will ask which of the motivation models named in the PREASSIGNMENT STUDENT PREPARATION section feature(s) all four of these types of variables and what the significance of this is.

4.  Your instructor will now give each small group the following materials: a large sheet of dark-coloured cardboard, two pads of sticky notes, a marker and a small supply of masking tape and will assign a section of classroom wall space to each group. One member of each group will then tape the sheet of cardboard to the wall (in landscape fashion). Your group's task is to build your own model of motivation. For this exercise, you will be restricted to the variables used in the five motivation models you reviewed in the PREASSIGNMENT PREPARATION section. You must make every attempt to include all four types of variables in your model.

5.  Print the names of each of the four types of variables in large capital letters on the blue sticky notes (one variable per sticky note) and place each note in the appropriate position on the sheet of cardboard.

6.  Next, reach consensus in your group on the dependent variable(s) for your model i.e., choose a dependent variable (or variables) from any of the five motivation models you reviewed in preparation for this exercise. (You may choose more than one dependent variable but remember that your model must be able to be tested.) Print the name of each dependent variable on a different yellow sticky note and place it in an appropriate position on the sheet of cardboard.

7.  Choose the independent, intervening and moderator variables and continue to build your model by printing the variable names on the yellow sticky notes and placing them on the sheet of cardboard. You are welcome to move the sticky notes around as you develop your model e.g., your group may change any of its decisions/choices at any point in the model-building process. For example, your group may decide to make a certain intervening variable into a moderator variable or an intervening variable into an independent variable, etc. Of course, you will need a solid rationale for all the decisions/choices you make during the model-building process.

8.  When you have completed your motivation model, check to make sure your model meets the criteria of a good theory and a good motivation model as articulated in Step 3. above. Further, discuss how you would proceed to test your model.

9.  Your instructor will ask each group in turn to present its model of motivation and plans for testing the model.

**DEBRIEFING:**

1. Why are there so many different motivation models presented in any given organizational behaviour textbook?

2. What constitutes a good theory? A good motivation theory?

3. Which was the best model of motivation presented in class today (besides the one created by your group, of course)? Please explain your answer with reference to the class-determined criteria for a good theory.

4. Outline the steps in the research process that would be taken to test your group's model.

5.   What research publications and/or data bases would be the most useful for the literature review step in your research plan?

6.   What are the advantages and disadvantages of restricting the small groups in this exercise to variables already researched in the five well-known models of motivation?

7.   If you had not been restricted in this exercise to using variables from the five motivation models, what other variables would you have liked to include in your model of motivation? Please explain your answer.

## 22.  I'M SO SMART:
## WRITING PERSONAL GOAL STATEMENTS AND
## USING THESE TO TRACK PERFORMANCE

 **LEARNING OBJECTIVES:**

1.    To teach you the "how tos" and "whys" of writing personal goal statements using the SMART format.

2.    To give you the opportunity to track your performance using the SMART format.

## TYPE OF EXERCISE:

Individual activity and class-wide discussion

## RELATED CONCEPTS:

- Goal setting
- Management by objectives
- Performance management

 **TIME:** 20 minutes

Individual students will typically require 10 minutes to complete step 1. of the PROCESS/INSTRUCTIONS section. The debriefing will require an additional 10 minutes.

## BACKGROUND:

Goal setting can be a complex process for people in both work and personal situations. Individual goal setting is an important and integral part of the larger process of setting organizational objectives. The Management By Objectives approach, popularized by management theorist Peter Drucker, focuses all organizational effort toward the realization of shared goals. The first step is the review of the organization's objectives. The objectives for the individual worker are set in congruence with the organization's focus. Progress toward goal attainment is assessed regularly and worker performance reviews are tied to the achievement of these goals. Rewards are provided based on the level of goal achievement.[1]

Organizational researcher and consultant, Kenneth Blanchard, has devised a model that helps to narrow the focus when it comes to individual goal setting. His SMART model emphasizes that goals must be: Specific, Measurable, Attainable, Relevant and Trackable (HR practitioners prefer to operationalize this as Time-related).[2]

This exercise will teach you how to set SMART goals and give you practice in tracking your performance using the SMART model.

## PREASSIGNMENT STUDENT PREPARATION:

1.   Before the class in which you will complete this exercise, think about an assignment (an examination or a project for this course or another) that you must complete during this semester.

2.   Please complete the following "Writing a SMART Goal Worksheet" in order to establish a SMART goal for your project. Next, make a photocopy of your completed Worksheet. Be prepared to hand one copy to your instructor in class.

---

## WRITING A SMART GOAL WORKSHEET

Name:_____

Student Number: _____

Assignment or Project to Be Completed:_____

Date of Completion of this worksheet : _____

Please answer the following questions about your assignment/project. This process will lead to you the development of a goal related to this assignment/project.

1.   SPECIFIC

     a.   Describe the nature of the assignment/project you want to complete.

b. What do you want to achieve by completing this assignment/project?

2. **MEASURABLE**

  a. What information is available to you to track your success as you work on this assignment/project?

  b. How will you know when the assignment/project is complete?

  c. What criteria will you use to measure the success of this assignment/project?

3. **ATTAINABLE**

  a. Is the successful completion of this assignment/project realistically attainable in the current environment?

  b. What are some obstacles to your success in completing the assignment/project successfully?

   c.      What must be done to overcome these obstacles?

## 4.    RESULTS ORIENTED

What will be the outcome(s) of the successful completion of this assignment/project?

## 5.    TIME-RELATED (TRACKABLE)

When will the assignment/project be completed?

## 6.    YOUR SMART GOAL

In the space below write your SMART goal using the information accumulated in steps 1.-5. above.

---

**PROCESS/INSTRUCTIONS:**

1.  Your instructor will ask you if you had any difficulties in completing the "Writing a SMART Goal Worksheet" as directed in the PREASSIGNMENT STUDENT PREPARATION section and will encourage you to ask any questions you may have on the process. Your instructor will ask you to hand in a copy of your completed Worksheet.

2.  Over the duration of this course, track your progress in meeting the SMART goal you set for yourself at the end of the Worksheet.

3.  At various times throughout the course, your instructor will ask you to evaluate your progress toward meeting your SMART goal. At the end of the course, your instructor will ask you to engage in individual reflection on the extent to which you have achieved your SMART goal.


**DEBRIEFING:**

1.  As a class, discuss the process of setting a goal for your project using the SMART approach. How does this approach differ from other goal setting approaches you have used in the past? In what ways is this approach similar to other goal setting approaches?

2.  Do you think that the goal you set using the SMART process is more attainable than a goal you might have set using a different process? Less attainable? Please explain your answer.

3.      How and where could the SMART goal process be used in a work organization?




4.      How could the  SMART goal process be used with an assignment group in a school setting or with a project team or work group in a work organization? What would be the difference between negotiating shared goals in a group setting and setting individual goals.




5.      What does the motivation research literature indicate about effectiveness of goal setting in general?




6.      What are the advantages of an effective goal setting process in work organizations? What factors can sabotage a goal setting session or process in a work setting?

## REFERENCES:

1.  Certo, Samuel C., Sales, Carol A. and Owen, Frances A. (1998). *Modern Management in Canada. (Canadian Seventh Edition).* Scarborough, Ontario: Prentice Hall Canada, pp. 127-128.

2.  Lankford, M.D. (1993, August). The Race Against Time. *School Library Journal, 39,* 5-10.

## 23. WITH THANKS:
## IDENTIFYING REWARD AND RECOGNITION ITEMS VALUED BY VARIOUS DEMOGRAPHIC GROUPS WITHIN WORK ORGANIZATIONS

 **LEARNING OBJECTIVES:**

1.  To introduce you to the challenges of developing specialized reward and recognition packages for various demographic groups within the workforce.

2.  To demonstrate the link between motivation theory and compensation practices.

**TYPE OF EXERCISE:**

Small group activities and class-wide discussions

**RELATED CONCEPTS:**

-   Rewards and recognition
-   Compensation
-   Demographic groups in the workforce
-   Career stages and development

 **TIME:** 50 minutes

The three career stage groups will typically require 20 minutes to review their interview data and to organize their findings into a class report. The class reports by career stage and debriefing will take another 15 minutes each.

## BACKGROUND:

David Foot and Daniel Stoffman[1] have described the characteristics of the Canadian generation cohorts born in the twentieth century. By now, most of the World War I generation (born between 1915 and 1919), the Roaring Twenties generation (born between 1920 and 1929) and the relatively small Depression Baby generation (born between 1930 and 1939) have all retired from the workforce. The World War II babies (born between 1940 and 1946), a relatively larger cohort than the Depression Baby cohort before them, felt a competitive squeeze but managed to prosper overall. The next cohort, the Baby Boomers generation (born between 1947 and 1966), was notable for its shear size.

In 1959, at the height of the boom, 479 000 babies were born in Canada. This very high birth rate, coupled with large increases in immigration, produced a generation that formed one third of Canada's population in the mid 1990s. However, it is a mistake to consider the Baby Boomers as one large, unified demographic. Life has been more prosperous for the members of the leading edge of the baby boom than it has been for the so called Generation X (or Gen-X) group born between 1960 and 1966. Gen-Xers are the people who have had to compete with those just a few years older who have benefited from the expansion in the 1970s and 1980s. The leading edge Baby Boomers occupy most of the higher rungs on the corporate ladder, blocking the way for the Gen-Xers. In fact, the Gen-Xers have had to cope with life-long overcrowding which has prompted them to become mistrustful of large institutions and which has taught them instead to become self-reliant. Many Gen-Xers have had to live with their parents well into adulthood because of low employment rates and the high cost of housing. What has made their lives even more complicated is conflict with their World War II generation parents who have been very successful themselves and do not understand why their children cannot pull themselves up by the bootstraps and get to work.

The late Baby Boom Gen-Xers were followed by the Baby Bust generation (born between 1967 and 1979). This comparatively smaller generation, especially its younger members, are enjoying brighter economic prospects than the Gen-Xers. Such prospects have freed the Baby Bust generation to be more idealistic than the cash-strapped Gen-Xers.

The Baby Boom Echo generation were born between 1980 and 1995. The front end of the Boom Echo group will most likely have more opportunities than the later-born Echos, known as Gen X-II. However, Gen X-II young people will have the understanding of their Gen-X parents who faced similar employment challenges.

The Millennium generation born between 1995 and 2010 is expected to be a relatively small cohort. This may well be another favoured generation faced with fewer competitive challenges than the two X generations before it.[2]

Understanding this pattern of boom and bust over the generations is important for HR professionals who are expected to develop meaningful and effective reward and recognition strategies that will appeal to members of the various generations at any given time in their work organizations. For example, the leading edge Baby Boomers like hierarchies and enjoy seeking

104

promotions within them, work a standard nine-to-five work week and look forward to a comfortable retirement at age sixty-five or sooner. In contrast, the Gen-Xers are more computer literate than the older Boomers, work on contracts rather than in the full time jobs, dislike (or are at best are indifferent) to hierarchies and "expect to work until they die, but take long sabbaticals throughout.[3]

Don Tapscott has labelled the older Baby Busters, the Echo generation and the leading edge of the Millennium generation the Net Generation since "...it is the first to grow up surrounded by digital media."[4] Tapscott believes that the Net Generations' comfort with digital technology will be its defining feature. He describes the Net Generation as "...is exceptionally curious, self-reliant, contrarian, smart, focussed, able to adapt, high in self-esteem, and has a global orientation."[5]

Aside from the influences of the demographic generation to which an employee belongs, a person's interests and reinforcers change as a function of career stage. There are three general career stages: early, middle and late. The early stage is characterized by the identification of critical career anchors which are the perceptions we have of our abilities, our values and the needs we hope to fulfill through work. In the middle stage, workers reevaluate their status as they face decreasing promotional opportunities and job alternatives. At this stage, an individual may choose to maintain the status quo, take advantage of career development interventions offered by their organizations or change careers entirely. Some people decide to start their own business. In the late stage, an individual is involved in planning for succession and for retirement.[6]

This exercise will give you the opportunity to explore the different HR strategies for reward and recognition that are most effective with different generations and at different career stages.

 **MATERIALS NEEDED:**

- One copy of the interview format and a consent form (as distributed by your instructor).
- One transparency sheet and one marker for each career stage group

## PREASSIGNMENT STUDENT PREPARATION:

1. Your instructor will assign you to a group of three students. You will also be assigned one of the three career stages (early stage, middle stage and late stage). With your group members, identify someone you know who you believe is in your assigned work stage and seek permission from that person for an interview.

2. Before the interview, brainstorm rewards, recognition mechanisms, incentives, etc. that you expect someone in your assigned and career stage/generation would be likely to value. Write three additional questions for the interview format to "test your hunches" i.e., the importance of these rewards/recognition mechanisms/incentives to your interviewee.

3.      Conduct the interview using the format provided by your instructor (augmented with your own three questions (see step 2. above). Be sure to ask your interviewee to sign the Consent Form at the end of the interview. This will allow you to use the information you collect for discussion in class. The interview can be conducted on the telephone or in person.

## PROCESS/INSTRUCTIONS:

1.      Your instructor will divide the class into three groups, one for each of the assigned career stages i.e., early stage, middle stage and later stage. Each interview group will join others in the class who were assigned the same career stage in the PREASSIGNMENT STUDENT PREPARATION section.

2.      In your larger career stage group, pool all the information gathered during the interviews to create a list of all the "rewards/recognition mechanisms/incentives" that would be most meaningful and effective for persons in this career stage/generation. Record this list on an overhead transparency sheet.

3.      Your instructor will ask each career stage/generation group to report in turn in the following order: late career stage, middle career stage and early career stage.

## DEBRIEFING:

1.      What rewards/recognition mechanisms/incentives were mentioned most in the interviews by each career stage/generation?

2.	What are the rewards/recognition mechanisms/incentives that are most meaningful and effective for you? Do you think others who were born in your same "generation" would offer the same list as yours? Please explain your answer.

3.	How meaningful is the concept of demographic "generations" to HR professionals in work organizations? Are there any weaknesses in such an approach? Please explain.

4.	Speculate on the rewards/recognition mechanisms/incentives list for the Millennium generation as they pass through each of the three career stages.

5.	How would you expect the career stages differ between Canada (a country with mandatory retirement) and the United States (a country without mandatory retirement)?

## FOLLOW-UP ACTIVITIES:

1.      Continue the research you have begun in this exercise by discussing with members of your family and friends about the rewards/recognition mechanisms/incentives that they value most in their work life.

2.      Do some extended research on the topic of mandatory versus non-mandatory retirement policies in three countries other than Canada and the United States.

## REFERENCES:

1.      Foot, D.K. and Stoffman, D. (1996). *Boom, Bust & Echo: How to Profit from the Coming Demographic Shift*. Toronto: Macfarlane Walter & Ross.

2.      Ibid.

3.      Bingham, R. and McCullough, M.(1998, November). Rebels with a business plan. *The Globe and Mail Report on Business Magazine*, pp. 77-88.

4.      Louder Echo: The Net Generation; http://www.growingupdigital.com/Lecho.html

5.      Ibid.

6.      Greenberg, J., Baron, R.A., Sales, C.A., and Owen, F.A. (1996). *Behaviour in Organizations*. Scarborough, Ontario: Prentice Hall Canada, pp. 211-215.

# 24. DIFFERENT STROKES FOR DIFFERENT OCCUPATIONAL GROUPS: DESIGNING SALIENT REWARDS AND RECOGNITION FOR INDIVIDUALS IN DIFFERENT OCCUPATIONAL GROUPS

 **LEARNING OBJECTIVES:**

1.      To identify salient financial and non-financial rewards and recognition components for individuals in different occupational groups.

2.      To investigate the reward and recognition strategies of contemporary Canadian organizations for different occupational groups.

## TYPE OF EXERCISE:

Invited panel and class-wide discussion

## RELATED CONCEPTS:

- Rewards and recognition
- Positive reinforcement
- Shaping
- Organizational behaviour modification
- Motivation
- Needs theories
- Compensation and benefits
- Recruitment and selection

 **TIME:** 45 minutes

The panel presentation and questions will require a maximum of 30 minutes. The debriefing will require an additional 15 minutes.

 **MATERIALS NEEDED:**

- One copy of the "Rewards/Recognition Strategies Comparison/Contrast Sheet" (supplied by your instructor).

## PREASSIGNMENT STUDENT PREPARATION:

1.  For this exercise, your instructor will be inviting a panel of managers from some of the following different types of organizations: hospitals/nursing homes, call centres, retail sales and manufacturing to come to class and discuss financial and non-financial reward and recognition strategies used in their organizations. The target occupations will be some or all of the following: nurses, order takers (call centres), sales associates, and machine operators. To prepare for the class in which you will be listening to the panel, search the Internet or daily newspapers for job ads for the above named target occupations (and/or others identified by your instructor).

2.  Speculate on the types of financial and non-financial rewards and recognition that might be currently in vogue in the various organizations and for the target occupations. Bring your notes to class.

3.  Please answer the questions:

    - How much should and how can organizations tailor their reward and recognition strategies to suit the individual differences of employees?

    - How can organizations tailor their reward and recognition strategies to suit the individual differences of employees?

## PROCESS/INSTRUCTIONS:

1.  At the beginning of class (before the introduction of the panel), your instructor will hand out a worksheet on which you will be able to make notes during the panel presentation. Next, your instructor will ask each panelist to introduce herself or himself and give a brief profile of her/his organization and the related target occupation.

2.  Your instructor will then ask the panelists to describe the financial and non-financial reward and recognition strategies used in their organizations for the different target occupational groups. Make notes on the worksheet given to you at the beginning of the class as the discussion progresses.

3.	When all the panelists have made their presentations, you will be allowed to ask the panelists questions for a period of 10 minutes.

4.	After the brief question period, the panelists will be thanked by the instructor and be excused from the class.

## DEBRIEFING:

1.	Were there any surprises for you in the panelists' information?

2.	What were the most salient types of reward and recognition for each occupational group? Which needs were the different strategies targeting?

3.	How aware did the panelists seem to be about individual differences within each occupational group? Give examples of reward and recognition strategies mentioned by the panelists that you felt accounted for individual differences and others that you felt ignored individual differences.

4.     Of all the financial and non-financial rewards and recognition strategies mentioned which appealed the most to you? The least to you? Please explain your answers.

**FOLLOW-UP ACTIVITIES:**

1.     Write a class letter to the panelists thanking them for sharing their time and information with you.

2.     Write a job ad for each of the target occupation in which you point out the potential rewards and recognition in "your organization".

## 25. DOWN WITH WALLS AND FUZZY CUBICLES: REDESIGNING WORK SPACE TO IMPROVE PRODUCTIVITY

 **LEARNING OBJECTIVES:**

1. To research the relationship between productivity and physical space/interior design.

2. To discover and investigate open environment designs in use in Canadian organizations.

3. To give you the opportunity to design a "new office" with the following ends as guidelines: increased team interaction and creativity enhancement.

## TYPE OF EXERCISE:

Group Internet research, small group activities, proposal presentation to a panel and class-wide discussion

## RELATED CONCEPTS:

- Work space design
- Office design for the 21st century
- Productivity
- Creativity
- Team interaction
- Motivation
- Knowledge workers

 **TIME:** 70 minutes

The four bidder groups and the judge group will be given 15 minutes in total at the beginning of class to prepare for the proposal presentations. The proposal presentations will require 6 minutes for each group (5 groups in total = 30 minutes) to present and 3 minutes for the answering of the judges' question (5 groups X 3 minutes = 15 minutes). The debriefing will take an additional 10 minutes.

## BACKGROUND:

Everyone from Dilbert to top business executives have turned their attention in recent years to the potential link between productivity and work space design. On the cynical side, Dilbert plays up the evils of the infamous fuzzy cubicle office design. In a more hopeful vein, 90 percent of the 200 business decision makers surveyed by the American Society of Interior Designers perceived that improving interior design can boost productivity.[1]

While few would be so naive as to assume that furniture alone could unlock the door to increased productivity, even the greatest skeptics would have to take a second look at the impressive results achieved by some Canadian and American companies that have experimented with new office design, such as Digital Renaissance (Toronto),[2] Amoco Production Co. (Denver) and Ethicon Endo-Surgery Inc. (a Cincinnati-based division of Johnson & Johnson)[3], Cossette Communication Marketing (Montreal), and Nortel (the Nortel Brampton Centre)[4] David Dunn, Nortel's director of global workforce planning redesign the work space, not only redesigned a huge, empty former manufacturing factory, but also created a "colorful, energetic, horizontal, self-contained city" complete with two main streets, smaller pathways leading to colour-coded neighbourhoods (departments), seven indoor parks, one Zen garden, a bank, fitness and wellness centres, basketball and volleyball courts, a physiotherapy clinic, a dry-cleaning service and a number of cafés and restaurants.[5]

The "drivers and enablers of change" in office design are many. Changing worker demographics, increasing volatility in global marketplaces, and the explosion of new technologies are forcing "a re-thinking of work and the workplace". The hallmarks of knowledge work are: multi-disciplinary teams, communication, creativity, flexibility, and continuous learning.[6]

This exercise will give you the opportunity to draft a competitive proposal for work space redesign for a workforce of knowledge workers.

 **MATERIALS NEEDED:**

- Audio-visual equipment (reserved by groups in advance of this class)
- Three sheets of flip chart paper and one marker for each small group
- One roll of masking tape

## PREASSIGNMENT STUDENT PREPARATION:

1. Your instructor will assign you to one of five groups in advance of the class in which you will be completing this exercise. One group will be designated as "Judge" and the other four groups will be designated as "Bidder" and will be given an identification number e.g., 1, 2, 3, etc. During the exercise in class, the bidder groups will each be making a proposal for office space redesign for a Canadian advertising agency to the panel of judges (actually they are executives from the ad agency). The ad agency executives have

purchased a very large, empty former warehouse which they want to turn into office space.

2.   Both the judge and bidder groups will research the topic of "office design" on the Internet. The groups should pick a time and place suitable for all members to do the research together. Please visit the following web sites (and more if time allows):

- http://www.fastcompany.com/online/16/nortel.html
- http://www.digital-ren.com
- http://www.cossette.com
- http://www.steelcase.com/knowledge_researchhtml/workevo_center.html
- http://www.steelcase.com/knowledge_researchhtml/unwopr_center.html
- http://www.steelcase.com/knowledge_research/organize.html
- http://www.steelcase.com/knowledge_research/workexp.html

3.   The bidder groups will search through the newspapers for original copies of Dilbert cartoons (and/or other work-related cartoons) which focus on work space design (especially the infamous fuzzy cubicles!). As part of your proposal for the panel of judges, you will put together a collage of three cartoons. Your collage will help you prove that a change in office design is needed.

4.   The bidder groups will need meet at least one additional time to plan out their proposal for the panel of judges. Be sure to plan out your audio-visual requirements and to order the necessary equipment (with your instructor's prior approval) for the class. You will be given an additional 15 minutes in class to polish your proposal presentation. Your presentation must not exceed 6 minutes.

5.   The judge group will also explore the Internet sites listed in Step 2. above but will not be preparing a cartoon collage. The bidder groups will be presenting their proposals for office redesign to you in class. After all, you are executives from the ad agency. You will be choosing the winning proposal. You will need to discuss the criteria you will be looking for in a winning design proposal. You will ask each bidder group one question following its presentation i.e., a different question for each group. Your instructor will chat with you during the 15 minute period in class when the bidder groups are polishing their proposals.

**PROCESS/INSTRUCTIONS:**

1.   **For the bidder groups:** Within your small group, take the next 15 minutes to polish your 6 minute office design proposal. Be sure the audio-visual equipment you reserved for the class has arrived and is in good working order. Remember to start your presentation with your short cartoon collage of original cartoons showing the cynical side of office design today. Your purpose is to win the contract for the redesign of the empty warehouse the ad agency has purchased. Only one proposal will win.

**For the panel of judges:** You will spend the next 15 minutes showing your Internet research materials, reviewing your criteria, rehearsing your questions for the bidder groups and consulting with your instructor.

2.  Your instructor will determine the order of the proposal presentations by lottery and will act as the official timer for the presentations. The presentation will end at the 8 minute mark (ready or not!). The answer to the one question asked by the judges to the each bidder group after its presentation must not exceed 3 minutes. Again, your instructor will be the timer.

3.  The judges will announce their decision and their rationale at the beginning of the next class.


## DEBRIEFING:

1.  Do you believe that work space design for knowledge workers affects their productivity? Please explain your answer with reference to the information you found during your Internet search and/or evidence presented in class during this exercise.

2.  What additional factors (beyond furniture and equipment placement) could make or break your new work design?

3. What features of workplace design presented in the proposals would particularly appeal to you if you were a knowledge worker in the ad agency? Please explain your answers.

## FOLLOW-UP ACTIVITIES:

1. Design a research study that would prove that the winning work space redesign proposal has affected productivity in the manner hoped by management (after one year in use).

2. Redesign your classroom into a "dream learning space". Give complete rationale for your proposal.

## REFERENCES:

1. Proper, E. (1998, June 8). Surroundings affect worker productivity. *Industry Week*, p. 11.

2. Greenberg, J., Baron, R.A., Sales, C.A. and Owen, F.A. (2000). *Behaviour In Organizations*. Second Canadian Edition. Scarbourough, Ont.: Prentice Hall Canada, pp. 226-227.

3. Wah, L. (1998, May). The Power Office. *Management Review*, pp. 10-15.

4. Chadderton, L. (1998, August). Nortel Switches Cities. *Fast Company*, pp. 112-114.

5. Ibid., p.113.

6. Cornell, P. and Baloga, M., Work evolution and the new "office"; http://www.steelcase.com/knowledge_researchhtml/workevo_center.html

## 26. FROM BOTH SIDES NOW?:
## LIVING WITH A MOBILITY CHALLENGE

 **LEARNING OBJECTIVES:**

1.  To sensitize you to the frustrations facing people who have mobility challenges.

2.  To help you to become a more astute observer of physical barriers in the work environment.


**TYPE OF EXERCISE:**

Individual activities (out-of-class) and class-wide discussion


**RELATED CONCEPTS:**

*   Diversity
*   Individual differences
*   Work space design

 **TIME:** 30 minutes

The class will require 15 minutes each to complete the charts and to debrief.


**BACKGROUND:**

While there is some evidence in recent years of increasing emphasis in government legislation and company policies on avoiding discrimination on the basis of special needs, the functional realities do not yet match the rhetoric. For people who do not have difficulty with mobility, a cursory inspection of most public buildings and corporate work spaces in Canada would suggest that they are easily accessible. Ramps, wide door ways, lowered elevator control panels demonstrate the increasing commitment to improve accessibility. However, closer inspection, especially from the vantage point of a person sitting in a wheelchair, often reveals quite a different story.

This exercise will give you an opportunity to experience the challenges that people who have mobility difficulties have to cope with every day.

 **MATERIALS NEEDED:**

- One wheelchair for every five students in the class. The wheelchairs must be available to students for a minimum of one day each during the week before this exercise is discussed in class.
- Small note pad and pen supplied by each student
- Four flip charts and four marking pens

## PREASSIGNMENT STUDENT PREPARATION:

1. Your instructor will assign you to a group with four other students. During the week before you will be discussing this exercise in class, you and your group members will take turns spending one day each in the wheelchair. Be sure your day in the wheelchair falls on a day when classes are in full swing at your school and that on your day in the wheelchair, you take a least one full tour of your school. During the time you are using the wheelchair, you will follow your regular routine. You may decide to work in pairs with one other group member taking notes and pushing the wheelchair (only when asked).

2. Keep a diary of your one day's experience in the wheelchair. Note the following: the positive events and emotions during the day, the moments of frustration or other strong negative emotions, the accessibility barriers and the ways those who are walking interact with you (or avoid interacting with you).

## PROCESS/INSTRUCTIONS:

1. In class, your instructor will ask for four volunteers to record the results of the out-of-class activities. Each recorder will be stationed at a different flip chart. Each flip chart will display a different title e.g. Chart 1: Positive Events/Emotions; Chart 2: Frustrations/Negative Emotions; Chart 3: Accessibility Barriers (plus subheadings: At School; At Home; and In The Community) and Chart 4: Personal Interactions (plus subheadings: Eye Contact; Physical Distance; Other).

2. Next, your instructor will poll individual class members about their experiences in the wheelchair. She or he will ask each student for one point in round robin fashion until the essence of the experience has been shared and each chart has received due attention.

**DEBRIEFING:**

1.      What did you learn as a result of your one day in the wheelchair?

2.      Reflect on the information recorded on four charts. What surprised you? What did not surprise you?

3.      If your university or college were to hire your class as an accessibility consultation group, what changes would you recommend your school make to its physical plant? What "sensitivity training" would you recommend for college or university staff, faculty and students?

**FOLLOW-UP ACTIVITIES:**

1.      Visit a facility that provides services primarily for persons (children and/or adults) who have mobility challenges. Notice all specially-designed features of the physical plant that make it easily accessible and comfortable for people who are using wheelchairs, walkers, canes and other assistive devises. Interview the staff trainer in this facility about the way in which the organization prepares its staff to respond to the needs of its clients/consumers.

2.     Visit web sites that provide information: 1. about assistive devices and services for people who have mobility challenges (for example, http://www.excite.com/guide/health/disabilities?search=accessibility+and+disabilities or http://www.activeliving.ca/activeliving/alliance/alliance.html) and 2. about Canada's "National Strategy for the Integration of Persons With Disabilities, Industry Canada's Assistive Devices Industry Office (ADIO), ADIO's projects, and the Assistive Devices Industry Association of Canada (http://strategis.ic.gc.ca/SSG/as00011e.html).

3.     Write a class (or individual) report which outlines your day in a wheelchair experience and recommendations and submit the report to Human Resources department at your school.

## 27. THAT WAS FAST AND YOU DON'T EVEN KNOW ME!: THE SELECTION INTERVIEW AND DECISION

 **LEARNING OBJECTIVES:**

1.    To give you the opportunity of making a selection decision.

2.    To stimulate your thinking about the important role played by interviewing skills in gathering rich information upon which to base a sound selection decision.

3.    To have you appreciate the folly of making important selection decisions based on scant information about the candidate.

## TYPE OF EXERCISE:

Individual activities in "bear pit" fashion, class-wide participation and discussion

## RELATED CONCEPTS:

- •    Recruitment and selection
- •    Selection decision
- •    Interviewing skills

 **TIME:** 55 minutes

Choosing the interviewers, getting them established at the front of the room and having them brainstorm the required competencies for the position to be filled will typically require 15 minutes. Canvassing the rest of the class for additional competencies will require an additional 5 minutes. The distribution of the interview material and the first vote of the interviewers will require 10 minutes. The reading of the interview information to the class and the interviewers second vote is expected to take an additional 10 minutes. The class vote, the tally and recording of all three voting sessions and the receipt of further information by the instructor and the debriefing will take 15 minutes.

## BACKGROUND:

Like all important, nonprogrammable decisions, the selection decision should be based on as much rich and relevant information as possible. While researchers have questioned the validity of the employment interview and 201 HR professionals, in a 1996 survey, gave the employment interview a slightly above average rating i.e., a rating of 3.49 and 3.42 for unstructured interviews and structured interviews respectively on a 5-point scale (with "5" reserved for an "extremely good" method for producing the best employees and a "1" for a method that was "not good"), one of the most popular selection methods continues to be the one-to-one employment interview.[1,2]

Employers believe that the interview in any of its various face-to-face forms e.g., nonstructured, structured, situational, behavioural description interview, or panel interview can be a potential source of rich information provided, among other factors of course, that the interviewer has the skills required. Poor interviewers, for example, waste too much of the interview time talking and not enough time in actively listening and truly getting to know the candidate. While the interviewer must spend some time giving an overview of the organization and explaining the requirements of the position, he or she must encourage the candidate to talk at length so that the interviewer can assess how that candidate might fit with the position and, further, how that candidate might add value to the organization and mesh with the corporate culture. If the interviewer lacks the requisite questioning techniques and/or active listening skills, the quality (and likely, also the quantity) of the information base for the final selection decision will be less than useful and will inevitably contribute to a poor selection decision.

This exercise will take the form of a mock interview in which the interviewer is forced to make a final selection decision based on less than rich information.

 **MATERIALS NEEDED:**

- Five 4" by 6" white index cards, each with a different letter of the alphabet printed on it
- One roll of masking tape
- A small box or a hat filled with slips of white paper each containing a tidbit of information about the candidate (supposedly revealed by the candidate in a recent interview)
- 10 blank ballots (2 each for the five interviewers)
- Five pens
- A set of two 3" by 5" index cards (one green and one pink) for each student in the class who is not playing the role of an interviewer

## PROCESS/INSTRUCTIONS:

1. Your instructor will ask for five volunteers from the class. The five volunteers will then be asked to sit in chairs at the front of the room. For the purposes of this exercise the five volunteers will play the role of independent interviewers i.e., each interviewer will complete the task without talking to any of the other interviewers. Each interviewer will be given a letter of the alphabet as an identifier. The task for the interviewers will be to weigh certain bits of information that supposedly were revealed to the interviewer in a recent face-to-face interview with the candidate. The position the interviewers are trying to fill is a senior leadership position in a large-sized manufacturing company which is in dire need of a turnaround.

2. Your instructor will ask the interviewers to brainstorm a list of the competencies that they would expect a candidate for such a position to have. A volunteer from the rest of the class will be asked to write the list on the chalkboard. Before declaring the list as final, your instructor will invite the rest of the class to add any other competencies they wish to the list.

3. Each of the five interviewers will be asked to choose three pieces of paper at random from the set prepared by the instructor. These pieces of paper each contain one "bit of information" which supposedly was obtained by the particular interviewer in a recent meeting with candidate. Each interviewer must not share these bits of information with anyone else in the room. The interviewer will then consider this information in the light of the nature of the position to be filled and of the competencies listed on the chalkboard. The interviewers will then be given a pen and a "ballot" by your instructor. Within the time limit set by your instructor, each interviewer will render a selection decision by writing the word "accept" or "reject" on the ballot, their interviewer identifier letter and the number "1". Your instructor will first collect these ballots and then ask each interviewer in turn to read out his or her three bits of information without revealing his or her selection decision. After each interviewer has read out his or her bits of information, the interviewers again will be asked to record a selection decision (this decision may or may not be the same as the first) in the same manner as before and to write a "2" on this ballot along with his or her identifier letter. Again, your instructor will collect these ballots.

4. Before announcing the decisions reached by the individual interviewers, your instructor will ask the rest of the class to render a selection decision which will be equivalent to the interviewers' second decision. This vote will taken by asking the rest of the class to hold up one of the two index cards they were given: a green index card means "accept" and a"pink" index card means "reject". Your instructor will record the results of this vote on the chalkboard..

5. Your instructor will now tally the interviewers' ballots and record the results by interviewer for each vote on the chalkboard. Your instructor will give you further information on the candidate.

**DEBRIEFING:**

1.      Think back over your own employment interviews. Did you ever feel that an interviewer you encountered lacked the necessary interviewing skills? What did he or she do that convinced you of this lack?

2.      Do you agree or disagree with the following statement: "Employment interviewers are in the first instance really searching for negative information rather than positive." Please explain your answer.

3.      What is particularly realistic about this exercise? What makes this exercise seem somewhat unreal?

4.      What are the potential costs of poor interviewing skills for an organization?

5.      What are the advantages and disadvantages of the one-to-one employment interview as a selection method?

6.      What are the advantages of using a computer interview as a complement to the face-to-face interview? In your opinion, will the computer interview ever replace the face-to-face interview. Please explain your answer.

**FOLLOW-UP ACTIVITIES:**

1.      Do some research using the Internet and other electronic databases available by modem from your library on the topic of the employment interview, specifically:

- What role is played in the interview by nonverbal communication?
- How far into the interview does the interviewer get on average before he or she establishes a reject or accept bias?
- How important is physical appearance in the employment interview in today's job market?

2.      Compile two lists of references on the "how tos" of the employment interview i.e., one from the interviewer's perspective and the other from the candidate's point of view.

**REFERENCES:**

1.  Tepstra, D. (1996). *The Search For Effective Methods*. In Belcourt, M., Sherman, A., Bohlander, G. and Snell, S. (1999). *Managing Human Resources*. Second Canadian Edition. Toronto: ITP Nelson, p.173.

2.  Murray Axsmith and Associates. (1997). In Belcourt, M., Sherman, A., Bohlander, G. and Snell, S. (1999). *Managing Human Resources*. Second Canadian Edition. Toronto: ITP Nelson, p. 198.

## 28.  IF I KNEW THEN WHAT I KNOW NOW: DISCRIMINATION IN THE EMPLOYMENT INTERVIEW

 **LEARNING OBJECTIVES:**

1.    To increase your knowledge of the "Prohibited Grounds of Discrimination in Canada".[1]

2.    To sensitize you to permissible and prohibited questions to ask candidates during the employment interview.

**TYPE OF EXERCISE:**

Individual Internet search, small group activities and class-wide discussion

**RELATED CONCEPTS:**

- Legal issues in HR
- Discrimination
- Canadian Human Rights Act
- Human Rights Codes for Canadian provinces
- Employment interview

 **TIME:** 45 minutes

Small groups will typically require 20 minutes in total to share their Internet search results and to complete the chart of questions. The class presentation and discussion of the questions will require 15 minutes. The debriefing will require another 10 minutes.

## BACKGROUND:

The Canadian Human Rights Act entitles all individuals to equal employment opportunities without regard to: race or colour, national/ethnic origin, religion, age, family/marital status, sex (including pregnancy or childbirth), pardoned conviction, disability (either physical or mental or as the result of dependence on alcohol or drugs), or sexual orientation.

Section 8 of the Act reads:

> It is a discriminatory practice,
>
> (a)     to use or circulate any form of application for employment, or
>
> (b)     in connection with employment or prospective employment, to publish any advertisement, or make any written or oral inquiry
>
> that expresses or implies any limitation, specification or preference based on a prohibited ground of discrimination.

This Act covers employment in federal jurisdiction. Included are the various federal government departments and agencies, Crown corporations, airlines, banks, railways, interprovincial pipelines, radio, television and telephone companies that do business in more than one province.[2] The Canadian provinces have established their own Human Rights Codes under the umbrella of the Canadian Human Rights Commission.

This exercise will expand your knowledge of the prohibited grounds of discrimination in Canada in general and in your province in particular.

 **MATERIALS NEEDED:**

- Two sheets of flip chart paper and one marker for each small group
- One roll of masking tape

## PREASSIGNMENT STUDENT PREPARATION:

Before the class in which you will be completing this exercise, search the following sites for information on human rights and the employment interview:

1.     The Canadian Human Rights Commission (http://www.chrc.ca/ http://www.chrc.ca/prohibit-motifs.asp?l=e and http://www.chrc.ca/screen-preselection.asp?l=e)

2.   The Human Rights Commission of your own province and that of any one other province from the following list:

- Alberta: http://www.albertahumanrights.ab.ca/
- British Columbia: http://www.bchrc.gav.bc.ca/
- Manitoba: http://www.gov.mb.ca/hrc/
- New Brunswick: http://www.gov.nb.ca/hrc-cdp/e/index.htm
- Nova Scotia: http://www.gov.ns.ca/just/hr.htm
- Ontario: http://www.ohrc.on.ca  and http://www.ohrc.on.ca/english/publications/emp_app_forms_eng.htm
- Prince Edward Island: http://www.gov.pe.ca/case/human/index.asp
- Quebec: http://www.cdpdj.qc.ca/
- Saskatchewan: http://www.gov.sk.ca/skrc/

3.   The Ontario Human Right Commission (http://www.ohrc.on.ca/  and http://www.ohrc.on.ca/index2.htm)  Click on  "Teaching HR in Ontario". (Many of the other Canadian provinces have similar packages.) The package includes an HR quiz, Fact Sheets, eight case studies and discussion questions. On the same page you will find a link to the "Teachers Package". Click on this and you will learn the answers to the questions posed in the "Teaching HR in Ontario" package.

Please make notes and bring them to class.

## PROCESS/INSTRUCTIONS:

1.   Please read the following scenario:

*You are, Petra, a recent college graduate. Your area of concentration in college was computer science. You were delighted last year to have landed a job at a large Canadian radio station. Now, one year later, the owner/operator has asked you to assume some additional HR related duties because of your excellent "people skills". The station is desperate to fill the receptionist's position at the front desk. An ad for the position was placed in the newspaper three days ago and already you have a long list of candidates to interview. Since this is your first recruitment and selection assignment and you were not trained in HR in college, you are quite nervous about the upcoming employment interviews. To make matters worse, on the news today you heard about a complaint being lodged against the owner of another radio station in your province for violating the Human Rights Code during the employment process. You decide to call a friend from college who majored in HR to get some advice on what questions to ask and which to avoid during the interviews.*

2. Your instructor will divide the class into small groups. Share in general with your group the information you found during your search of the Internet (see the PREASSIGNMENT STUDENT PREPARATION section above) on the topic of Human Rights in Canada and the provinces.

3. Everyone in your small group will take the role of Petra's HR friend. (The radio station is located in your province.) You offer to sit and draft the questions with her. On a sheet of flip paper (turned in the landscape mode-you will need at least two sheets), write the following headings, one under the other, at the extreme left of the paper: age, religion, criminal record, disabilities, national/ethnic origin, height and weight, country of birth, religion/creed, family status and sexual orientation. To the right of this list, divide the rest of the paper into two equal columns. Label the first column "Prohibited Questions" and the other column "Permissible Questions". Please complete the chart by writing one permissible question (if there is one) for each of your headings on the left of the paper.

4. Your instructor will ask each group to read its questions under certain headings. After each set of questions is read other groups are free to critique what they have heard.

## DEBRIEFING:

1. Have you or anyone you know ever felt discriminated against during the employment process? What did you do (or what did the other person do) about the discrimination?

2. Is there much discrimination in Canada? What evidence can you cite for your answer?

3.     What are the best resources for someone like Petra to learn about human rights issues in Canada?

## REFERENCES:

1.     Prohibited Grounds Of Discrimination In Canada; http://chrc.ca/prohibit-motifs.asp?l=e Reproduced with the permission of the Minister of Public Works and Government Services Canada.

2.     A Guide To Screening and Selection In Employment; http://www.chrc.ca/screen-preselection.asp?l=e

## 29. UP CLOSE AND PERSONAL ON THE CULTURAL MOSAIC: UNDERSTANDING HOW YOUR OWN CULTURAL HISTORY SHAPES YOUR WORK-RELATED VALUES AND ATTITUDES

 **LEARNING OBJECTIVES:**

1.      To increase your awareness of your own culture and its work-related values.

2.      To understand how your cultural history shapes your work-related values and attitudes.

## TYPE OF EXERCISE:

Individual activities and class-wide discussion

## RELATED CONCEPTS:

*       Diversity
*       Work-related values and attitudes
*       Team

 **TIME:** 15 minutes

The class will typically require about 15 minutes to debrief.

## BACKGROUND:

Diversity awareness is a concept that is gaining increasing importance in a shrinking world. Globalization in all fields increases the interaction of members of all cultural backgrounds. This interaction presents not only enormous and opportunities but also difficult challenges. Managers everywhere are continually trying to find ways for people with very different work-related values, attitudes and traditions to work together effectively and efficiently.

Understanding other cultures must start with understanding your own. Many people may work hard to understand other cultures without first consciously examining the beliefs with which they grew up. For those who have limited contact with people who belong to other cultures, the notion of studying one's own culture may seem rather like studying the air we breathe. However, without an awareness of the biases to which we have been acculturated, it is difficult for us to understand our reactions to other cultures and the accommodations we must make to work effectively with members of other cultures.

This exercise will help you to focus on your culture's attitudes toward various aspects of work life.

## PREASSIGNMENT STUDENT PREPARATION:

Interview family members from as many generations as possible. Also interview people whom you identify as being leaders of your cultural community. Interviews may be conducted in person, on the telephone, by e-mail or by mail. Use the following questions to start your interviews and add questions that are suggested to you by the responses you receive. The goal of the interview is for you to learn about the work-related values and attitudes that are held by members of your family and cultural group.

## INTERVIEW QUESTIONS

- **VOCATIONAL CHOICE:**

  - How did you decide your career?
  - Who in your family influenced your career decision most?
  - What kinds of work did you not considered because your family and your community would have disapproved?
  - What kinds of work does your family and community value most?

- **THE GENDERS AND WORK:**

  - When you were growing up, what were the expectations of men and women in terms of work life?
  - What jobs were considered inappropriate for men and what jobs were considered inappropriate for women?
  - What changes have you seen in your career in the way that men and women work together?
  - What would your parents and grandparents have said about these changes?

- **TEAMS AT WORK:**

  - Describe your first experience working in a team at work.
  - How were group membership and group leadership determined for the team?
  - What changes have you seen during your career in the way that teams work together?

- **WORK-RELATED RULES:**

  - What were the most important messages/rules about work that your family and your community gave you as you were growing up?
  - Were there sayings that were used frequently that conveyed a message to you about how a person should work?


**DEBRIEFING:**

1.  Reflect on the impact that your cultural history has had on the work expectations you have for yourself and others.

2.  What information discussed in the interviews was most surprising to you? How does this information explain your work-related values and attitudes?

**FOLLOW-UP ACTIVITIES:**

1.    Compare interview findings with a classmate who is a member of your cultural group. Notice the similarities and differences in the cultural messages you were given through the interviews.

2.    Compare interview findings with a classmate who is a member of a different cultural group. Notice the similarities and differences in the cultural messages you were given through the interviews.

## 30. GUESS HOW MUCH WE MISSED YOU LAST WEEK: IDENTIFYING THE COSTS OF ABSENTEEISM AND RECOMMENDING STRATEGIES TO REDUCE COSTS

 **LEARNING OBJECTIVES:**

1.      To raise your awareness of the costs of absenteeism.

2.      To give you the opportunity to identify both the hard and soft costs of absenteeism.

3.      To give you some hands-on experience in recommending strategies for attendance management.

## TYPE OF EXERCISE:

Individual activities, small group activities and class-wide discussion

 **TIME:** 40  minutes

The class as a whole will require 10 minutes to share their research on absenteeism/attendance management. Small groups will require 15 minutes to analyze and make their recommendations for Shams. The debriefing is expected to take another 15 minutes.

## BACKGROUND:

The skyrocketing costs of absenteeism in work organizations across Canada is a matter of great urgency for management. Like voluntary turnover, absenteeism is a form of employee withdrawal. Absenteeism has been linked in the research literature with both low job satisfaction and low organizational commitment[1] but the strength of these relationships have been found to be modest. This suggests that there are many and various other reasons for absenteeism from work. HR can build business cases that highlight improved management practices as a way to reduce absenteeism and to increase job satisfaction.

 **MATERIALS NEEDED:**

- Three sheets of flip chart paper and one marker for each small group
- One calculator for each small group
- One roll of masking tape

## PREASSIGNMENT STUDENT PREPARATION:

In preparation for the class in which you will be discussing this exercise, do some Internet research on the topic of absenteeism/attendance management. In particular, attempt to answer the following questions:

- What are the estimated annual costs of absenteeism for work organizations in Canada? In the United States?
- What are the reasons for absenteeism in Canadian work organizations?
- What strategies have been proposed in the management literature for attendance management i.e., to reduce absenteeism?

Your instructor will suggest some web sites to get you started. Bring a summary of your findings and a list of web sites and research sources to class.

## PROCESS/INSTRUCTIONS:

1.   Your instructor will ask you to share your Internet research findings with the class as a whole by asking each of the questions assigned in the PREASSIGNMENT STUDENT PREPARATION section. Three student volunteers will be chosen to capture the main ideas from the research on the chalkboard i.e., one student will note all cost-related information, another will note the reasons for absenteeism and the third will note strategies for reducing absenteeism.

2.   Your instructor will divide the class into small groups. Please read the following scenario:

   *Shams graduated two years ago from a Canadian post-secondary institution. His major was business administration. For personal reasons, he decided to take a job in his home town with a small non-unionized company (80 employees). This company which grows, sells and distributes potted plants is beginning to make quite a name for itself in Canada and has begun to export to the United States. Shams is one of the three telephone order takers in this company. He is becoming increasing bored with the work. In the last six months, Shams has been absent six*

138

*Fridays. His supervisor, Mary Henhawk, is not a pleased with his attendance record. The two other order takers are complaining about the extra work and stress that Shams' absences are causing for them. Mary is well aware that each order taker handles on average $10 000 in sales per day.*

3.  In your group, calculate the dollar value of Shams' absences. Note your answer on the sheet of flip chart paper. Make a list of other costs associated with the absences of Shams. Again, note your list of associated costs on the same sheet of flip chart paper. On the another sheet of paper, brainstorm a list of possible reasons for Shams' absences. On a third sheet of paper, recommend strategies for his supervisor, Mary Henhawk to use with Shams.

4.  Your instructor will ask the groups in turn to share their work on the costs, reasons for absences and attendance management strategies.

## DEBRIEFING:

1.  In your opinion, what was the single best attendance management strategy suggested for Shams? Please explain your answer.

2.  What role should disciplinary action play in Shams' case?

3.  What are the hard and soft costs associated with absenteeism in work organizations?

139

4.      What are the most effective strategies in general for attendance management?

5.      What training do supervisors need with regard to attendance management?

6.      How would attendance management strategies differ in a unionized company versus a non-unionized company like Shams'?

## FOLLOW-UP ACTIVITIES:

1.      Simulate an initial fact-finding meeting between Mary Henhawk and Shams where Mary is genuinely interested in learning "what's up" with Shams and why he has been away so much on Fridays.

2.      Develop a disciplinary action plan for Mary Henhawk to use with Shams (in case she decides on this route). Next, alter the same plan for use in an unionized company which is otherwise similar to Shams'.

## REFERENCE:

1.      Greenberg, J., Baron, R.A., Sales, C.A. and Owen, F.A. (2000). *Behaviour In Organizations*. Scarborough, Ont.: Prentice Hall Canada, pp. 175-176.

# 31. THEY'RRRREEE OFFFF AND RUNNING: HELPING NEW EMPLOYEES TO BECOME PRODUCTIVE QUICKLY

 **LEARNING OBJECTIVES:**

1.      To heighten your awareness of the costs of not having an effective orientation program.

2.      To sensitize you to the range of information new employees need to know as they start a new job.

3.      To give you an opportunity to plan a new employee orientation program.


**TYPE OF EXERCISE:**

Small group activities and class-wide discussion


**RELATED CONCEPTS:**

•       New employee orientation
•       Recruitment and selection
•       Management accountabilities

 **TIME:** 70  minutes


The small groups will require 10 minutes to share their positive and negative orientation stories and to make their choice of the one best story in each category. The reports of the stories to the class will require 10 minutes. The sharing of the written materials completed by and collected by the small groups will take 15 minutes. The orientation plan and report to the class will require 15 minutes and 10 minutes respectively. The debriefing will require an additional 10 minutes.

## BACKGROUND:

Many organizations have learned over time about the many cost-effective advantages of a well-thought out and executed orientation program for getting their new-hires "out of the gate" with a "fast start".[1] "Employee orientation provides new employees with basic background information about the employer, information they need to perform their jobs satisfactorily. ... Orientation programs range from brief, informal introductions to lengthy, formal programs."[2]

The following (and often much more) is covered with the new employee during an effective orientation process: information on the company such as key personnel, mission, vision, philosophy and values, personal information of interest to the new employee such as introduction to his/her supervisor and team members, benefits information, reporting procedures on a variety of topics e.g., time sheets, overtime, sick days, the rules of behaviour and conditions of employment e.g., hours of work and pay schedule, training overview and schedule and security and safety information e.g., keys and lockup procedures, safety procedures and rules.[3,4] "An orientation program [or the lack of one] can make an immediate and lasting impression on an employee that can mean the difference between the employee's success or failure."[5]

In most organizations, the HR function takes the lead in the orientation process. However, for a truly effective orientation program, a cooperative effort between line and staff is vital.[6] The benefits most often cited from an effective, formal orientation program are the following: lower turnover, increased productivity, improved employee morale, lower recruiting and training costs, facilitation of learning and reduction of the new employee's anxiety.[7]

This exercise will give you an opportunity to think through the entire orientation process and to plan an orientation program.

 **MATERIALS NEEDED:**

* Two sheets of flip chart paper and one marker for each small group (for use outside of class)
* One roll of masking tape
* Two transparency sheets and one marker for each small group (for use in class).

## PREASSIGNMENT STUDENT PREPARATION:

Before the class in which you will be completing this assignment, you will need to complete several activities as an individual and as part of a small group. Your instructor will assign you to one of six small groups.

As an individual, you need to complete the following tasks before class: 1. Interview any two relatives asking them to recall a couple of positive and a couple of negative experiences about their first two weeks on any job e.g., what did the company (and its members) do (and/or not do) to help these people "get with the program" fast as they started their new jobs and 2. Recall your own positive and negative experiences with your first days on a job. Make notes on these stories and bring your notes to class.

Your instructor will assign a task for each group to complete before class:

---

- **Group 1:**     Visit your school's HR department and obtain any information you can about the orientation process in place for new employees, in particular for departmental secretaries (or "administrative assistants" as some are called). Ask for a copy of any written material on the orientation process including the "Employee Handbook" (if such exists). Make a summary of the steps in the orientation process and list the information included for the new employee. The summary should be recorded on a sheet of flip chart paper. Bring the completed flip chart paper to class. Be sure the names of your group members are printed on the flip chart paper.

---

- **Group 2:**     Obtain a copy, read and summarize the following articles (or parts thereof as specified):

1.     Birchard, B. (1997, September) Hire great people fast, *Fast Company, pp. 132-143*. Also available on *Fast Company*'s web site: http://www.fastcompany.com Search for "orientation". Summarize pp. 142-143 re: "Get a Fast Start". The article outlines orientation ideas from Cisco's Fast Start program and MEMC Electronic Materials (orientation as a self-managed project) - both US companies.

2.     Mieszkowski, K. (1998, February: March) Get with the program, *Fast Company*, pp. 28-30. Also available on *Fast Company*'s web site: http://www.fastcompany.com. Search for "orientation". Summarize the whole article. The article outlines orientation ideas from the electronic card company: Greet Street and from the well-known company Intel two more American companies.

The summary should be recorded on a sheet of flip chart paper. Bring the completed flip chart paper to class. Be sure the names of your group members are printed on the flip chart paper.

---

- **Group 3:** Obtain, read and summarize the following:

  1. Dessler, G., Cole, N, and Sutherland, V. (1999) *Human Resources Management In Canada*. Scarborough, Ont.: Prentice Hall Canada, pp. 301-302. On p. 301 you will find an orientation checklist from a retail chain and on p. 301, you will find a short feature on Toyota's orientation (and socialization) process at the Cambridge, Ontario plant. Be sure the names of your group members are printed on the flip chart paper.

  2. Belcourt, M., Sherman, A., Bohlander, G. and Snell, S. (1999). *Managing Human Resources*. Second Canadian Edition, Toronto: ITP Nelson, p. 214. Here you will find a supervisory orientation checklist.

  The summary should be recorded on a sheet of flip chart paper. Bring the completed flip chart paper to class. Be sure the names of your group members are printed on the flip chart paper.

---

- **Group 4:** Visit the HR department of a large manufacturing company and obtain any information you can about the orientation process in place for new employees, in particular for secretaries, (or "clerical" or "office employees" as some are called). Ask for a copy of any written material on the orientation process including the "Employee Handbook" (if such exists). Make a summary of the steps in the orientation process and list the information included for the new employee. The summary should be recorded on a sheet of flip chart paper. Bring the completed flip chart paper to class. Be sure the names of your group members are printed on the flip chart paper.

---

- **Group 5:** Visit the HR department of a large hospital and obtain any information you can about the orientation process in place for new employees, in particular for secretaries, (or "clerical" or "office employees" as some are called). Ask for a copy of any written material on the orientation process including the "Employee Handbook" (if such exists). Make a summary of the steps in the orientation process and list the information included for the new employee. The summary should be recorded on a sheet of flip chart paper. Bring the completed flip chart paper to class. Be sure the names of your group members are printed on the flip chart paper.

---

- **Group 6** Visit the HR department of any large organization (not an educational organization, a manufacturing organization or a hospital) and obtain any information you can about the orientation process in place for new employees, in particular for secretaries, (or "clerical" or "office employees" as some are called). Ask for a copy of any written material on the orientation process including the "Employee Handbook" (if such exists). Make a summary of the steps in the orientation process and list the information included for the new employee. The summary should be recorded on a sheet of flip chart paper. Bring the completed flip chart paper to class. Be sure the names of your group members are printed on the flip chart paper.

## PROCESS/INSTRUCTIONS:

1. In your small group, each student will outline the positive and negative stories of the orientation experiences of their relatives and of their own orientation experience. Your group will then choose one positive story and one negative story to share with the class.

2. Your instructor will ask each group in turn to share one positive and one negative orientation story (decided in Step 1. above). After each story, the class will be given an opportunity to comment.

3. Your group will now tape its completed flip chart sheet on the chalkboard and display nearby any written materials obtained during the completion of the task. Your instructor will ask each group in turn to present its materials to the class.

4. In your small group, mindful of the positive and negative stories you have heard in this class today and the results of the groups research findings, plan a new (or in your view, an improved) orientation program for secretaries/administrative assistants in your school. Summarize your plans on a transparency sheet.

5. Your instructor will ask a spokesperson from each group to outline the group's plan.

**DEBRIEFING:**

1.  What are the benefits of an effective orientation program for a new employee and for the company?

2.  What are the costs of a poor (or nonexistent) orientation program for new employees and for the company?

3.  What surprised you most about the negative stories about orientation told in class?

4.  Who should be responsible for a new employee's orientation? Who should be actively involved in the orientation process for a new employee? What role should each play?

5.    What were some of the best orientation ideas or plans you heard in class today? Explain why you think these are (or would be) effective?

**REFERENCES:**

1.    Birchard, B. (1997, September). Hire great people fast. *Fast Company,* pp. 132-143.

2.    Dessler, G., Cole, N, and Sutherland, V. (1999). *Human Resources Management In Canada.* Scarborough, Ont.: Prentice Hall Canada, p. 300.

3.    Ibid., pp. 301-302.

4.    Belcourt, M., Sherman, A., Bohlander, G. and Snell, S. (1999). *Managing Human Resources.* Second Canadian Edition. Toronto: ITP Nelson, p. 212.

5.    Ibid., p. 213.

6.    Ibid., p. 213.

7.    Ibid., p. 212.

# 32. THE "ELEGANT CURRENCY" OF MENTORING: LOOKING AT MENTORING FROM ALL SIDES

 **LEARNING OBJECTIVES:**

1.    To facilitate your investigation into the topic of mentoring as a career development tool.

2.    To learn the advantages of mentoring for both mentors and protégés.

3.    To learn the potential pitfalls in mentoring programs.

4.    To discover the "tricks of the trade" of mentoring by amassing your own virtual library.

## TYPE OF EXERCISE:

Individual Internet research, small group activities, and class-wide discussion

## RELATED CONCEPTS:

- Mentoring
- HR development
- Career development
- Learning
- Person-job fit
- Adult education

 **TIME:** 40 minutes

Small groups will typically require 15 minutes to consolidate their answers to assigned questions. The class-wide reporting of the answers will take 15 minutes. The debriefing will require an additional 10 minutes.

## BACKGROUND:

California-based organization consultant, Dr. Beverly Kaye, says today's mentoring is all about "learning to reciprocate" - as she calls it - "elegant currency". To demonstrate what she means, Dr. Kaye relates an example of the time a graduate student telephoned her asking if she would grant the student a 30-minute interview. In exchange for her time, the student offered her two hours of Internet research. The chance to fulfil each other's needs immediately got Dr. Kaye's attention.[1]

To Dr. Kaye, mentoring is a golden opportunity to learn from everyone in the company, not just those above in the hierarchy. "Mentoring is no longer just the grizzled old warrior having lunch a few times a year with the upcoming star. ... But in today's fast-paced and flatter companies, mentoring serves a host of other purposes, from retaining good staff to communicating across business lines."[2]

This exercise will give you the opportunity to explore the advantages and potential pitfalls of mentoring from the perspective of the organization, the mentor and the protégé.

 **MATERIALS NEEDED:**

- Three sheets of flip chart paper and one marker for each small group
- One roll of masking tape

## PREASSIGNMENT STUDENT PREPARATION:

Before the class in which you will be completing this exercise, your instructor will divide the class into small groups and will assign certain questions from the list below to each group. Each group member is expected to research the answers to her/his assigned questions on the Internet. Your instructor will give you a list of useful web sites to get you started. Please feel free to search for material beyond that found on the sites supplied by your instructor. The complete set of questions is as follows:

1. What is mentoring?
2. What are the purposes for which mentoring programs are established in organizations beyond career development?
3. What are the old myths and new realities of mentoring?
4. What is in it for mentors?
5. What is in it for protégés?
6. What roles do good mentors play?
7. What are the pitfalls that can sabotage mentorship programs in organizations?
8. Do men and women mentor differently?
9. Is "group mentoring" a viable option for contemporary organizations?

10. What are the keys to building a successful mentorship program in an organization?
11. Which companies have successful mentorship programs?
12. What web sites (excluding those given to you by your instructor) did you find were most informative on the topic of mentoring?

## PROCESS/INSTRUCTIONS:

1. In your pre-assigned small group, pool your answers to your assigned questions. Record a complete answer to each question on flip chart paper.

2. Your instructor will ask each group to present its answers in turn. As each group presents, its flip chart record will be posted on the chalkboard.

## DEBRIEFING:

1. What are the benefits to the organization, the mentor and the protégé of an effective mentoring program?

2. Why do some mentoring programs fail?

3.     What are the key elements of an effective mentoring program?

4.     How have mentoring programs changed over the years? Why have they changed?

5.     How does effective group mentoring work?

**FOLLOW-UP ACTIVITIES:**

1.     Find four other class colleagues who would like to experience mentoring first-hand. Meet together with your instructor and discuss the following:

- Who (a member of the HR profession) can you (the group) ask to be your mentor? How will you establish the first contact? What can you offer the mentor as your part of the "elegant currency"?

- What do you want to learn specifically from the mentor e.g., what the HR professional's job entails, how you might fit into the HR professional's world, how to work with other HR professionals in the HR department, etc.

- What structural guidelines do you suggest for the relationship e.g., how often you should meet together, how long should the relationship last, what expectations does each have for the other in the relationship, etc.

Your instructor will ask the group to make a report to the rest of the class on your group mentoring experience.

2. Invite representatives from a few companies/organizations which are operating successful mentoring programs at the present time to come to class to showcase their programs.

## REFERENCES:

1. Gibb-Clark, M., The Changing Face Of Mentoring; http://www.cybf.ca/insight/mentoring/articles/article.htm

2. Ibid.

# 33. GETTING TO KNOW ME:
## A PERSONAL PERSPECTIVE ON MANAGING STRESS

 **LEARNING OBJECTIVES:**

1.　　To increase your awareness of your approach to life stress.

2.　　To encourage you to develop a personal stress management plan.

## TYPE OF EXERCISE:

Individual activities and class-wide discussion

## RELATED CONCEPTS:

* Stress
* Stress management
* Self-evaluation

 **TIME:** 15 minutes (and up to 90 minutes outside of class)

The Internet questionnaires suggested for use in this exercise vary in length from 10 to 20 minutes each. Anyone who completes all four questionnaires and a stress management plan will need at least 90 minutes outside of class. The in-class debriefing will typically require 15 minutes.

## BACKGROUND:

Few people in North America are unaware of the increasing negative impacts of overwhelming stress. From role overload to technostress, people in all walks of life are bombarded with stressors. However, each individual reacts in his or her own way in response to stress. The first step in finding ways to manage stress is to become aware of your individual sensitivity to stress and stress coping strategies.

This exercise will introduce you to some Internet resources that will help you to examine whether you tend to be stress prone, how well you are coping with stress and whether your lifestyle is helping you to manage stress effectively. The web site on which you will find the questionnaires does not provide reliability or validity information about the instruments so it is not possible to report on the accuracy of the results they generate. In addition, the choice of language in some questionnaires may have different meanings from one region of the country to another. Some of the language used in the questionnaires may be offensive to some people.

## PREASSIGNMENT STUDENT PREPARATION:

1. Before the class in which this exercise will be discussed, visit the following web site: Personality Tests on the WWW (http://www.2h.com/Tests/personality.phtml)

2. Click on the links to the following questionnaires listed on the personality Tests on the WWW home page: Stress-O-Meter, Life Style test, Type A personality test, and Coping with stress inventory.

3. Complete each questionnaire. There is a button at the end of each questionnaire that refers you to the automatic scoring feature. Each questionnaire provides you with your score(s) and recommendations for managing your stress.

4. Make a note of your stress management strengths and weaknesses as identified in each questionnaire. Based on these questionnaire results develop a list of strategies you need to use to reduce your stress and to manage stress better.

## DEBRIEFING:

1. What did you learn about yourself during the completion of this exercise?

2.	How valid and reliable are the questionnaires you completed online? Why are these concepts important?

3.	Reflect on times in your life when you have felt most successful and in control of your life. What coping strategies were you using when you felt this way? Be sure to include these strategies in your new stress management plan.

4.	Discuss with your class colleagues, the stress management strategies that they find most helpful. Consider adding these strategies to your stress management plan.

**FOLLOW-UP ACTIVITIES:**

1.	Put your stress management plan into action for six weeks. At the end of that time complete the following questionnaires at http://www.2h.com/Tests/personality.phtml : Stress-O-Meter, Life Style test, Type A personality test, and the Coping with stress inventory. Compare the results from these questionnaires with the results you achieved the first time you completed them. The difference in your scores may reflect the impact of your stress management program.

2.	Ask your friends (outside of class) and your relatives about their stress management strategies. Adopt good ideas for your own stress management plan.

# PART 4

# GROUP
# PROCESSES

# 34. ALL FOR ONE:
## THE TUG OF WAR BETWEEN INDIVIDUAL PERFORMANCE GOALS AND TEAM EXPECTATIONS

 **LEARNING OBJECTIVES:**

1.  To illustrate potential conflicts between individual performance goals and effective team behaviour.

2.  To show how an organization's compensation system can, in fact, undermine the team values that a company wishes to promote.

**TYPE OF EXERCISE:**

Two-person group activities and class-wide discussion

**RELATED CONCEPTS:**

*   Team rewards and recognition
*   Culture
*   Compensation systems
*   Orientation of new-hires
*   Performance management

 **TIME:** 45 minutes

Students working in pairs will require 15 minutes to read, analyze and discuss their first assigned scenario. Students will require another 15 minutes to read, analyze and discuss the second scenario. The debriefing will typically require an additional 15 minutes.

## BACKGROUND:

Many contemporary Canadian organizations promote themselves as showplaces of such values as teamwork and collaboration. However, in actual fact, many of these same organizations ultimately design compensation systems that undermine the efforts of employees as they strive to achieve two different sets of goals set by management - both individual performance goals and team goals. Compensation systems, in effect, often inadvertently set up a tug of war between these two types of goals. This exercise illustrates the importance of designing compensation systems that actively support the team values espoused by organizations.

 **MATERIALS NEEDED:**

- Two scenarios (to be distributed by your instructor)

## PROCESS / INSTRUCTIONS:

1. You and all members of your class are employees in a large telemarketing company. This company has widely promoted its corporate culture as being solidly based on teamwork and collaboration. In fact, as employees, you and your class colleagues know that, in reality, your performance will be measured on both your individual contributions and on the achievements of your team.

2. Half the class will be given Scenario A to read, while the other half will be given Scenario B.

3. With a partner who has read the same scenario as you have (look for someone with a scenario printed on the same coloured paper as yours), discuss the following questions:

    - How would you feel if you were the agent living the situation described in the scenario?
    - What steps would you take to solve the dilemma you face?
    - What recommendations would you make to the organization to prevent other people from finding themselves in such a predicament?

4. Next, change partners and begin working with a person who has read the other scenario. Exchange scenarios. Based on the information contained in both scenarios, what would you and your new partner recommend to the organization to improve the situation described?

**DEBRIEFING:**

1.  Describe the feelings of "the two different agents" (at least as reported in class) in the scenarios. Explain why they felt this way.

2.  What recommendations would you now make to the organization to alleviate the conflicts between individual and team performance? (Be sure to relate your answer to compensation systems designed by the telemarketing organization.)

3.  Have you or any of your classmates found yourselves in a similar job situation? What did you do about it at the time? What would you do if you were in the same situation now?

**FOLLOW-UP ACTIVITIES:**

1.  Research compensation systems/incentive plans that other organizations use to encourage both individual and team performance in an organization.

2.  Develop a screening system that could be used by managers to evaluate whether their organization's individual and team performance goals are conflicting.

# 35.  BUILDING A FERRARI:
## EXTRAPOLATING TIPS FOR BUILDING HIGH PERFORMANCE PROBLEM-SOLVING TEAMS FOR GROUP ASSIGNMENTS

 **LEARNING OBJECTIVES:**

1.  To make you aware of different types of teams in the work organizations.

2.  To draw an analogy between the group assignments you have completed recently in school and team projects in work organizations.

3.  To underscore the difference between "group" and "team".

4.  To make you aware of the differences between effective teams and ineffective teams.

5.  To explore tactics for building high-performance teams in work organizations.

## TYPE OF EXERCISE:

Small group activities and class-wide discussion

## RELATED CONCEPTS:

*   Groups versus teams
*   Problem-solving teams
*   High-performance teams
*   Group development
*   Group decision making

 **TIME:** 50 minutes

The sharing of the initial success factors list in the small groups and across the class will typically require 15 minutes. The comparison of the groups' success factors and sharing with the class and the consideration of the TIPS factors not chosen and sharing with the class will take an additional 10 minutes each. The debriefing will require an additional 15 minutes.

# BACKGROUND:

Few individuals can avoid being part of a team as part of their work life. Whether the team is a temporary unit formed to complete a time-limited project or whether it is a permanent team, it is important for managers to know as much about the workings of teams as possible.

Firstly, managers and others must realize that a group is not automatically a team. A group may be defined as: "A collection of two or more interacting individuals with a stable pattern of relationships between them who share common goals and who perceive themselves as being a group."[1] In contrast, a team may be defined as "...a group whose members have complementary skills and are committed to a common purpose or set of performance goals for which they hold themselves mutually accountable."[2]

As Brian Dumaine pointed out in an article published in *Fortune,* companies far and wide have embraced the team concept. Well-known big companies such as Federal Express, Boeing, Nynex and IDS have reaped the benefits. One president confidently reported: "Your competitiveness is your ability to use the skills and knowledge of people most effectively, and teams are the best way to do that."[3] Further, Dumaine explains that there are a number of different kinds of teams used in work organizations e.g., problem-solving teams (knowledge workers who gather to solve a specific problem and then disband), work teams (empowered, self-managed teams that are formed to do the daily work), management teams (functional managers across different functions such as: marketing, design, and production, etc. who coordinate the work of the work teams), quality circles (supervisors and workers meet sporadically to work on problems of mutual concern in the organization) and virtual teams (members communicate by computer)[4].

Edward Lawler, a respected researcher in organizational behaviour, says: "People are very naive about how easy it is to create a team. ...Teams are the Ferraris of work design. They're high performance but high maintenance and expensive."[5] Teams need a lot of training and nurturing to become truly effective. Dumaine lists the following among the reasons why teams fail to reach their potential in companies: often companies form the wrong kinds of team, too often teams are "launched in a vacuum, with little or no training or support", many companies overuse teams, compensation packages have too often remained tied to individual performance rather than team performance, and the reengineering "craze" has damaged team spirit.[6]

This exercise will give you a chance to reflect on your own previous experiences with group and/or team performance and will introduce you to some strategies that can help to improve team performance in your next problem-solving team in school or at work.

 **MATERIALS NEEDED:**

- A copy of the "TIPS FOR BUILDING HIGH-PERFORMANCE TEAMS" handout material (one copy per small group to be distributed by your instructor)
- One sheet of flip chart paper and a marker per small group
- A roll of masking tape

## PREASSIGNMENT STUDENT PREPARATION:

Before the class in which you will completing this exercise, spend some time recalling a time or times when you were part of a "successful/effective" assignment group or problem-solving team in a work setting. Make notes about the experience(s), noting in particular, the composition ad nature of the group/team and those aspects which contributed to its success.

## PROCESS/INSTRUCTIONS:

1. Your instructor will ask the class to break into small groups. In your small group, discuss your successful group/team experience(s) and those of your group members. On the sheet of flip chart paper, list all the aspects of these groups/teams that made them successful.

2. Your instructor will ask each small group to share its group/team success factors with the class as a whole.

3. Next, your instructor will distribute a sheet entitled: "TIPS FOR BUILDING HIGH-PERFORMANCE TEAMS". Review these tips in your small groups. Compare your list of group/team success factors to the TIPS list. Put an asterix beside each item on your success factors list that matches an item listed on the TIPS list.

4. Your instructor will read each item on the TIPS list and a spokesperson for each group will raise his/her hand if this item was given an asterix by his/her group. Your instructor will note on the chalkboard those items on the TIPS list which were not chosen by the groups.

5. Your instructor will ask the small groups to consider those items from the TIPS list which were not chosen by any of the groups and to speculate on the reasons why these were not chosen.

6. Your instructor will read the list of TIPS not chosen and will ask the groups' spokespersons in round-robin fashion to give the reasons why the item was not chosen.

**DEBRIEFING:**

1.  Discuss the similarities and differences among the success factors lists generated by each small group before the TIPS material was handed out.

2.  Discuss the similarities and differences among the TIPS items chosen by the small groups overall after the TIPS material was handed out. Why were some of the items on the TIPS list not chosen?

3.  Extrapolate from the success factors lists generated by your class and the chosen TIPS list to compose a "TIPS FOR BUILDING HIGH-PERFORMANCE GROUP ASSIGNMENT TEAMS" list.

4.  What role can your instructor play in building high-performance group assignment teams in the future?

## FOLLOW-UP ACTIVITIES:

1.  Interview the leaders of successful teams in your university or college. These could be sports teams, debating teams, or teams formed in other areas of campus life. Ask them about their philosophy of team leadership. Reflect on the generalizability of these concepts to the world of work teams.

2.  Read the biographies of two successful team leaders. These may be business leaders, sports leaders, political leaders, religious or arts leaders who have been recognized in the media for building successful teams. Examine the similarities and differences in the skills used by these leaders.

## REFERENCES:

1.  Forsyth, D.L. (1983). *An Introduction To Group Dynamics.* In Greenberg, J., Baron, R.A., Sales, C.A., and Owen, F.A., (2000). *Behaviour In Organizations.* Scarborough, Ontario: Prentice Hall Canada, p. 230.

2.  Katzenbach, J.R., & Smith, D.K. (1993). The discipline of teams. In Greenberg, J., Baron, R.A., Sales, C.A., and Owen, F.A., (2000). *Behaviour In Organizations.* Scarborough, Ontario: Prentice Hall Canada, pp.259-260.

3.  Dumaine, B. The Trouble With Teams, *Fortune*, p. 86. Reprinted from the Sept. 5, 1994 issue of *Fortune* by special permission. Copyright 1994, Time Inc.

4.  Ibid., p. 87.

5.  Ibid., p. 86.

6.  Ibid., p. 87.

# 36.  ARE WE HAVING FUN YET?:
## UNDERSTANDING THE DIFFERENT STAGES
## IN THE DEVELOPMENT OF GROUPS

 **LEARNING OBJECTIVES:**

1.     To give you an opportunity to demonstrate your understanding of the five stages in the development of groups.

2.     To present the five-stage model of group development as a general framework.

**TYPE OF EXERCISE:**

Small group activity and class-wide discussion

**RELATED CONCEPTS:**

•      Stages in the development of groups

 **TIME:** 35  minutes

The five groups will typically require 10 minutes to plan their presentations and prepare the transparency. Group presentations and the debriefing will require 10 minutes and 15 minutes respectively.

## BACKGROUND:

Tuckman and Jensen[1] proposed the following general framework of group formation and development:

- **Stage 1 - Forming:** Group members come together, get to know one another, explore acceptable, preliminary ground rules with regard to the group's task (e.g., the level of productivity expected) and interpersonal relations (e.g., who is the group's leader). Feelings of confusion and uncertainty fade as members accept that they are bona fide members of the group.

- **Stage 2 - Storming:** Group members challenge the control exercised by the group's leader and show hostility towards one another. Conflict may escalate to a point where the group disbands or the conflict may be resolved. If the latter is the case, the group's leader is accepted at this point.

- **Stage 3 - Norming:** Group members adopt a set of ground rules and recognize a shared responsibility for the group's activities and outcomes. An esprit de corps begins to develop.

- **Stage 4 - Performing:** Group members concentrate on performing their task.

- **Stage 5 - Adjourning:** Once the group's purpose has been fulfilled the group dissolves. (Other less positive outcomes which will end the group may be: the number of group members dwindle or the group's norms outlive their usefulness or acceptability to group members.)

This exercise will give you the opportunity to gain a deeper understanding of the Tuckman and Jansen general model, to test its limits and to use it to help you understand the dynamics of your group/team projects in school and/or at work.

 **MATERIALS NEEDED:**

- One overhead transparency sheet and one transparency marker for each small group

## PROCESS/INSTRUCTIONS:

1.      Your instructor will divide the class into five groups. Each group will be assigned one of the stages in the Tuckman and Jensen general model: forming, storming, norming, performing, or adjourning.

2.      Brainstorm a list of characteristics including: feelings, actions, etc. that you think would typically be part of the make-up of your assigned stage. Plan a non-verbal presentation for the class in which your small group will demonstrate these various characteristics. List the characteristics (using words and phrases) on an overhead transparency.

3.      After each group makes its presentation (in the same order as the model), one member of the group will display his or her group's transparency and will answer any questions or challenges from the other groups.

## DEBRIEFING:

1.      How useful is the Tuckman and Jensen model: 1. To you as a student looking back over your many experiences with group assignments in school and 2. To a manager who is in the process of creating a team which will be assigned a complex and important task?

2.      Why was the Tuckman and Jensen model introduced in the BACKGROUND section as a "general framework"? What is the opposite of a "general framework"? Explain the implications of this discussion for the practical application of this model regardless of setting i.e., school or work.

3. Describe your best group assignment experience. Describe your worst group assignment experience. Apply the Tuckman and Jensen model as a general framework to each experience in an attempt to understand what went right or what went wrong.

4. What lessons can instructors who routinely give group assignments to their classes learn from your answer to Question 3. above and from the model itself?

**REFERENCE:**

1. Tuckman, B.W. & Jensen, M.A. (1977). Stages Of Small Group Development Revisited. In Greenberg, J., Baron, R.A., Sales, C.A., and Owen, F.A. (2000). *Behaviour In Organizations*. Second Canadian Edition. Scarborough, Ontario: Prentice Hall Canada, pp. 234-235.

# 37. MONKEY SAY, MONKEY SEE, MONKEY DO: A LESSON IN INTERPERSONAL COMMUNICATION

 **LEARNING OBJECTIVES:**

1.      To help you to explore the complexities of interpersonal communication.

2.      To improve your observation skills.

## TYPE OF EXERCISE:

Two-person group activities and class-wide discussion

## RELATED CONCEPTS:

*       Interpersonal communication
*       Verbal and nonverbal communication

 **TIME:** 30 minutes

The two-person activities will typically require 15 minutes. The class-wide debriefing will require an additional 15 minutes.

## BACKGROUND:

In an age dominated by e-mail and voice mail, we tend to focus our attention on verbal messages. While "word-smithing," both written and oral, is important in getting messages across, nonverbal communication is also a very significant mode of communication. We ignore nonverbal messages (or "body language") at our own peril. Without careful attention to these emotion-laden messages, we may miss the heart of the real message.

This exercise, based on work by famed family therapist Virginia Satir[1], encourages you to be more observant during interpersonal communication activities in your daily life.

## PROCESS/INSTRUCTIONS:

1.    Choose a communication partner for this exercise. Sit directly facing one another. You will take turns making a statement to your partner while your partner listens silently. The first person to speak makes a statement in his or her characteristic manner. The listening partner then repeats the statement mirroring the speaker's tone of voice, rate of speech, body posture, gestures and facial expression. Discuss the speaker's reaction to the listener's perception of his or her communication style. What aspect of the mirroring was most surprising for the speaker? What aspects of the speaker's communication style were most striking?

2.    Reverse roles. The first speaker now becomes the listener and mirrors the statement and nonverbal communication of the new speaker.

3.    Repeat this exercise so that each partner is speaker twice and listener twice. Discuss briefly after each speaking activity.

4.    Your instructor will ask for five volunteer speaker-listener pairs to share their experiences with the class as a whole.


## DEBRIEFING:

1.    What were the overall reactions from the speaker-listener volunteer pairs from Step 4. ? Did you and your partner react in a similar manner (assuming you were not one of the volunteer pairs to report to the whole class)?

2.    What aspects of nonverbal communication did you find most surprising in your speaker-listener activities?

3.	How important is nonverbal communication to effective interpersonal communication? Please explain your answer.

4.	How significant is the role played by nonverbal communication in today's world of global business?

5.	What are the best methods to use to teach a manager or team leader to be more effective in picking up nonverbal cues in interpersonal communication activities?

6.	Discuss what happens when a person simultaneously gives a verbal message and a different and competing nonverbal message. For example, suppose a person is feeling very nervous about undertaking a new project at work but is afraid to tell anyone about his or her discomfort. When asked, he or she says there is no problem undertaking the assignment but his or her body language and vocal tone are tense and suggest he or she would like to refuse the assignment. If you were the person to whom he or she reports and you picked up on the competing messages, what would you do?

**REFERENCE:**

1.    Satir, V. (1972). *Peoplemaking.* Palo Alto, CA: Science and Behavior Books, Inc.

# 38. MAYBE E-MAIL IS A BETTER BET:
## A DEMONSTRATION IN INTERPERSONAL COMMUNICATION

 **LEARNING OBJECTIVES:**

1.      To demonstrate distortions in interpersonal communication.

2.      To examine the challenges of maintaining accuracy in verbal communication.

## TYPE OF EXERCISE:

Class-wide activity and discussion

## RELATED CONCEPTS:

*       Interpersonal communication
*       Organizational communication

 **TIME:** 20 minutes

Depending on the size of the class, this exercise should take 10 minutes for the message passing activity and 10 minutes for debriefing.

## BACKGROUND:

Communication is filtered through individual perception. When we hear words, we do not simply store them away in a neutral fashion. We interpret them based on our perspective. Our perception of the meaning of the message tends to influence how we interpret the words and then pass them on to others. This reinterpretation of verbal messages contributes to many misunderstandings in the workplace.

This exercise, familiar to many as a childhood standard, is worth revisiting to keep you vigilant as a listener and as a communicator.

## PROCESS/INSTRUCTIONS:

1.    Your instructor will write a one sentence message on a piece of paper and then will whisper the same message into the ear of one member of the class.

2.    The message will be passed throughout the class by having the member of the class who first received the message then whisper the message into the ear of the next until the message has been passed from person to person throughout the entire class. Each person may say the message only once.

3.    The last person to receive the message announces it. Your instructor will write this on the chalkboard verbatim. Your instructor will hand the piece of paper which contains her/his original message to the last person who received the message from the class. This student will read the original message aloud. Your instructor will write this message above the "class" message on the chalkboard.

4.    The class will then discuss the reasons for the difference(s) between the original message and the "class" message.

## DEBRIEFING:

1.    Why was the "class" message different from the original message?

2.    What are the implications of the differences between the "two" messages for communication in work organizations?

3.   Would e-mail have been a better bet for the original message?  Please explain your answer.

4.   Compare the message-passing activity in this classroom to the passing of rumours in a work organization.

5.   As a manager, what communication strategies would you use to avoid the kind of distortion demonstrated in this exercise?

# 39. I CAN'T HEAR YOU IF I CAN'T SEE YOU: A DEMONSTRATION IN INTERPERSONAL COMMUNICATION

 **LEARNING OBJECTIVES:**

1.    To simulate certain messaging devices which are devoid of visual cues.

2.    To sensitize you to the importance of visual cues in interpersonal communication.

## TYPE OF EXERCISE:

A two-person activity and class-wide discussion

## RELATED CONCEPTS:

- Interpersonal communication
- Organizational communications

 **TIME:** 25 minutes

Depending on the size of the class, partners will typically require 15 minutes to demonstrate the face-to-face and back-to-back situations. The class-wide debriefing will require an additional 10 minutes.

## BACKGROUND:

Famed family therapist, Virginia Satir[1] developed a variety of exercises to help families to explore communication patterns and their impact on personal relationships. This exercise will raise your awareness of the importance of visual information in interpersonal communication.

**PROCESS/INSTRUCTIONS:**

1.      Choose a partner for this exercise. Arrange your two chairs so that they are back-to-back and no closer together than 20 cm.

2.      You and your partner will be seated in your chairs and proceed to carry on a conversation on any topic of mutual interest. Keep the conversation going until your instructor tells you to stop.

3.      When your instructor gives you the signal, rearrange your chairs so they are facing one another.

4.      You and your partner will again be seated in your chairs and resume your conversation until your instructor signals you to stop.

5.      Return your chair to its original position i.e., before the exercise began.


**DEBRIEFING:**

1.      Compare and contrast the experience of talking back-to-back with that of talking face-to-face.

2.      What extra factors are in play when communicating face-to-face as opposed to back-to-back?

3.	What messaging devices might be compared with the back-to-back situation? What are the strengths and weaknesses of such devices?

4.	As a manager, what would you suggest to make the messaging devices identified in Question 3. above more effective?

5.	Discuss the organizational implications of visual cues in interpersonal communication.

**REFERENCE:**

1.	Satir, V. (1972). *Peoplemaking*. Palo Alto, CA: Science and Behavior Books, Inc.

# 40. LET'S NOT BEAT AROUND THE BUSH: LEVELLING IN INTERPERSONAL COMMUNICATION USING "I" MESSAGES

 **LEARNING OBJECTIVES:**

1.      To sensitize you to the power in simple changes in language.

2.      To introduce you to the concept of "I" messages.

## TYPE OF EXERCISE:

Two-person activities and class-wide discussion

## RELATED CONCEPTS:

*       Communication style
*       Interpersonal communication

 **TIME:** 35 minutes

The two-person groups will typically require 10 minutes for each partner to rehearse the use of "I" messages. The class debriefing will require an additional 15 minutes.

## BACKGROUND:

One of the most difficult issues facing anyone who works with groups is getting to the heart of a disagreement. Family Therapist Virginia Satir identified four dysfunctional communication patterns that interfere with honest, direct interpersonal communication. The "Blamer" is the person who traditionally finds fault with anyone and everyone rather than engaging in honest self-examination. The "Placater" avoids conflict by attempting to please everyone. The "Distractor" uses strategies such as jokes, walking around, and changing the subject. The "Computer" (sometimes called the "Rational Analyzer") is dispassionate and distant in his/her communication style. This person tends to make distant, analytic statements about a situation without committing his/herself to a specific perspective.

Satir urged her clients to express their feelings using "I" statements that were clear, honest expressions of their feelings. In an organizational context for example, a person who is upset about the inconsistent contributions his or her colleague is making to a team project would be encouraged to "level" with that person by saying something such as "I feel very nervous when I don't know if you will have your work done on time" rather than blaming ("The fact we are late on this project is all your fault.") or placating ("It's OK. I'll look after the whole project") or Distracting ("Did you hear about the new romance in the IT department?") or Computing ("Research has shown that fifty percent of partnerships fail.").[1,2]

This exercise will give you practice translating inappropriate communications into levelling "I" statements.

 **MATERIALS NEEDED:**

- One coloured card for each student (either blue or yellow as distributed by your instructor)

**PROCESS/INSTRUCTIONS:**

1.  Choose a partner in the class with whom you will work on this exercise. This person must be holding a card that is a different colour from yours. Sit facing your partner.

2.  Think of a time when you have been very frustrated by a working or personal relationship. The person who has the blue card will start the exercise by making a series of statements about his or her frustration in the previous relationship using the ineffective communication styles described in the BACKGROUND section e.g., Blaming, Placating, Distracting or Computing. The person with the blue card will pause after each statement to give the person who has the yellow card the opportunity to express the same sentiment using an "I" statement. For example, if the person with the blue card says "You never show up on time and I am left wasting my valuable time," the person with the yellow card might say "I feel disrespected when you keep me waiting." The person with the blue card should make five statements, each one reframed by the person with the yellow card.

3.  Please switch roles and repeat Step 2. above i.e., the person with the yellow card will make five statements using ineffective communication styles. The person with the yellow card will pause after each statement to allow the person with the blue card to respond using levelling "I" statements.

4.  When you have each had an opportunity to complete both roles, discuss with your partner the difference in the experience of both delivering and receiving the messages delivered using the ineffective communication styles. Contrast this with the experience of sending and receiving the "I" messages.

**DEBRIEFING:**

1.      As a class, discuss the experience of using the ineffective versus the levelling forms of communication. How did it feel to blame, placate, distract or compute? How did it feel to hear those messages?

2.      How did it feel to send and receive "I" messages?

3.      Discuss strategies you could use as an HR professional to encourage employees to use "I" messages in their interpersonal communication at work.

**FOLLOW-UP ACTIVITIES:**

1.      Notice the communication styles used by your class colleagues and by your colleagues at work. Speculate on how the use of "I" messages would change the nature of these interactions.

2.      Keep a communication log by jotting down the number of times during a day that you use blaming, placating, distracting, computing and levelling when you are communicating with friends and colleagues.

## REFERENCES:

1.      Satir, V. (1972). *Peoplemaking*, Palo Alto, CA: Science and Behavior Books, Inc.

2.      Gladding, S.T. (1998). *Family Therapy: History, Theory and Practice.* Second Edition. Upper Saddle River, NJ: Prentice-Hall.

# 41. DECISIONS, DECISIONS:
# THE ANATOMY OF MANAGERIAL DECISION MAKING

 **LEARNING OBJECTIVES:**

1.    To give you the opportunity to examine what constitutes a good decision versus a bad decision.

2.    To investigate how managers make decisions in contemporary Canadian organizations.

3.    To highlight individual and organizational barriers to effective decision making.


**TYPE OF EXERCISE:**

Small group activities and class-wide discussion


**RELATED CONCEPTS:**

•    Decision making

 **TIME:** 45 minutes


The interviewing teams will typically require 15 minutes to discuss the interview results and to complete the two worksheets. The interviewing team reports will take 15 minutes. The debriefing will require an additional 15 minutes.


**BACKGROUND:**

Decision making is "the process of making choices from among several alternatives."[1] Making timely and effective decisions is a crucial skill for managers in any type of organization. In fact, some would say decision making is the most important of all managerial activities. Others would go so far as to say that managing is decision making.[2]

The traditional, analytical model of decision making breaks the process down into an eight-step process (albeit circular) namely: 1. Identifying the problem; 2. Defining the objectives; 3. Making a predecision (making a decision about how to make the decision e.g., to make the decision alone, to delegate it to someone else or to have a group make the decision; 4. Generating alternatives; 5. Evaluating the alternatives; 6. Making a choice among alternatives; 7. Implementing the chosen alternative; and 8. Monitoring the effectiveness of the decision e.g., was the problem solved?[3] Researchers are quick to point out that this is a general only not a prescriptive model.

This exercise will give you the opportunity to investigate how decisions are made by contemporary managers in your community, what constitutes a good versus a bad decision and what individual and organizational barriers stand in the way of effective decision making in organizations.

## PREASSIGNMENT STUDENT PREPARATION:

Before the class in which you will completing this exercise, your instructor will ask you to choose two partners with whom you will form a small interviewing team.

At the pre-interview meeting (outside of class), your group will draw up a list of relatives who are managers. From this list, your group will choose the one person they would most like to interview (and a second choice in case the first is unavailable within time frame outlined by your instructor). The member of your group who is related to the chosen manager will make the initial contact and will ask her or him to grant your interviewing team a 20 minute interview on how she or he makes decisions. Offer to fax your questions to the manager in advance for information purposes. Further, assure your manager that her or his name or the name of her or his company will not be mentioned at any time in class discussion and that this assignment does not involve a written report.

The following are the questions that your interviewing team will ask the manager:

1.      Please tell us about a time in your managerial career when you made a "good decision" about which you are still proud to this day.

- Please describe in general terms what the essence of the decision was.
- Would you describe this decision as a routine type of decision or a very complex type of decision?
- How did you go about making this decision? What were the steps you followed in making the decision? What kinds of information did you obtain and consider?
- Who else was involved in making this decision?
- Why do you regard it now as a good decision?

184

- In hindsight, would you have done anything differently in your decision making process e.g., involve anyone else, seek more information, etc.
- Did you ever have any formal training in how to make decisions?

2.  Please tell us about a time in your managerial career when you made a "not so good decision".

- Please describe in general terms what the essence of the decision was.
- Would you describe this decision as a routine type of decision or a very complex type of decision?
- How did you go about making this decision? What were the steps you followed in making the decision? What kinds of information did you obtain and consider?
- Who else was involved in making this decision?
- Why do you regard it now as a not so good decision? Can you identify any barriers to effective decision making (individual or organizational) that resulted in a not so good decision?
- In hindsight, would you have done anything differently in your decision making process e.g., involve anyone else, seek more information, etc.

3.  During the interview, all members of the interview team will take notes and will complete the two forms printed on the next page: 1. Decision Making Analysis Worksheet - Good Decision and 2. Decision Making Analysis Worksheet - Poor Decision. Be sure not to go over the 20 minute time limit for the interview (unless your interviewee invites you to stay longer). Also be sure to send a "Thank You" note to your interviewee signed by all members of the interview team as soon as you possibly can. Bring your notes on the interview to class. The student who "shared" her or his relative for this assignment will obtain a 3"x 5" index card from your instructor and will write on it the name, title, and complete mailing address for the interviewee. This student also will include on the index card her or his name and relationship to the interviewee.

# DECISION MAKING ANALYSIS WORKSHEET - GOOD DECISION

TYPE OF DECISION:

WHY GOOD DECISION:

STEPS IN THE INTERVIEWEE'S
DECISION PROCESS:

COMPARISON OF STEPS ABOVE
WITH THE TRADITIONAL MODEL:

CONTRAST OF STEPS WITH
TRADITIONAL MODEL:

DECISION MAKING TRAINING:

OTHER OBSERVATIONS:

# DECISION MAKING ANALYSIS WORKSHEET - POOR DECISION

TYPE OF DECISION:

WHY POOR DECISION:

STEPS IN THE INTERVIEWEE'S
DECISION PROCESS:

COMPARISON OF STEPS ABOVE
WITH THE TRADITIONAL MODEL:

CONTRAST OF STEPS WITH
TRADITIONAL MODEL:

BARRIERS TO EFFECTIVE
DECISION MAKING:

- INDIVIDUAL:

- ORGANIZATIONAL:

OTHER OBSERVATIONS:

 **MATERIALS NEEDED:**

- One 3"x 5" index card (supplied by your instructor) for each interviewing team

**PROCESS/INSTRUCTIONS:**

1.  Sit in class with your interviewing team. Your instructor will ask each group to report in turn on the good decision and then on the not so good decision. As you promised your interviewee, no one in your group will reveal the identity of your interviewee or that of her or his organization.

2.  Your instructor will ask the managers' relatives in class to hand in the completed index cards.

**DEBRIEFING:**

1.  Compare and contrast the decision making process outlined in the traditional, analytical model of decision making (please see the BACKGROUND section above) with the process actually followed by the interviewees. What do you conclude about the traditional, analytical model?

2.	For the majority of the interviewees, what distinguished the good decisions from the poor decisions?

3.	What were some of the individual and organizational barriers to effective decision making that were identified by the interviewees e.g., framing, heuristics, etc.?

4.	Did the type of decisions i.e., routine/programmed decisions versus nonprogrammed (complex) decisions play any particular role in decision effectiveness?

5.	How did the interviewees learn how to make decisions?

**REFERENCES:**

1. Greenberg, J., Baron, R.A., Sales, C.A., Owen, F.A. (2000). *Behaviour In Organizations*. Scarborough, Ontario: Prentice Hall Canada, p. 307.

2. Mintzberg, H. J. (1988). *Mintzberg On Management: Inside Our Strange World of Organizations*. New York: Free Press.

3. Wedley, W.C. and Field, R.H. (1984). *A Predecision Support System*. In Greenberg, J., Baron, R.A., Sales, C.A., and Owen, F.A. (2000). *Behaviour In Organizations*. Scarborough, Ontario: Prentice Hall Canada, pp. 305-307.

# 42. NOW YOU SEE ME NOW YOU DON'T: UNDERSTANDING AND USING THE NOMINAL GROUP TECHNIQUE AND DELPHI TECHNIQUE FOR PROBLEM SOLVING

 **LEARNING OBJECTIVES:**

1.      To introduce you to two methods for group decision making and problem solving, namely: the Nominal Group Technique and the Delphi Technique.

2.      To give you hands-on experience using one technique and an opportunity to observe the other.

**TYPE OF EXERCISE:**

Small group activities and class-wide discussion

**RELATED CONCEPTS:**

*       Group decision-making and problem-solving
*       Nominal Group Technique
*       Delphi Technique
*       Group process

 **TIME:** 45 minutes

The organization of the class into the NGT and Delphi groups will typically require 10 minutes. The decision task will take 20 minutes. The debriefing will require an additional 15 minutes.

191

## BACKGROUND:

Discussing issues in groups can be frustrating, time consuming and, for some, very intimidating. There are various group decision making techniques which offer an alternative from the ordinary face-to-face meeting. This exercise will examine two such techniques: the Nominal Group Technique (NGT) and the Delphi Technique.

NGT involves very little direct, open discussion, hence the term *nominal* group. The process involves the gathering of a small group to receive instructions. The problem is outlined and then participants write down their suggestions for problem resolution. These suggestions are then presented to the group and recorded on a chart by the group leader. When all the ideas have been recorded the group discusses each one. Finally, each group member ranks the solutions using individual secret ballots. The suggestion that receives the most votes becomes the group's chosen alternative.[1] The NGT can be used in a slightly modified distance format known as automated decision conferencing. This type of conferencing allows people in various locations to participate in a nominal group through teleconferencing or satellite distance conferencing.[2]

The Delphi technique does not require any face-to-face contact among group members. Instead, the group leader identifies a number of people who have considerable expertise in an area of special interest to his or her organization. The leader then contacts these people by letter, e-mail or fax to ask each person for his or her opinion about the best solution for the problem at hand. The leader then assembles all the suggestions and distributes the aggregated recommendations to all group members who, in turn, comment on the list. The leader examines these responses to see if a consensus has been reached. If it has then the organization has a direction to pursue to attack the problem. If not, then the leader redistributes the recommendations and comments until a consensus is achieved.[3]

This exercise will give you experience working with the NGT or Delphi approaches to group decision making and problem solving and an opportunity to observe the other technique.

 **MATERIALS NEEDED:**

- One copy of the Group Problem Sheet for each student in the class.
- One copy of the NGT Group Member Role Sheet for each member of a NGT group only
- One copy of the Delphi Group Member Role Sheet for each member of a Delphi group only.
- One copy of a Leader Role Sheet for the leaders of each NGT group leader and each Delphi group leader outlining his or her tasks.
- Four or six small pieces of paper (depending on the total number of small NGT and Delphi groups) for the instructor's use
- One roll of masking tape
- Four sheets of flip chart paper for each small group
- Four blank sheets of paper for each student in the class

## PREASSIGNMENT STUDENT PREPARATION:

Visit the web sites for any four colleges and/or universities of your choice. Go to the "Administration" page for each school, check the HR sections and notice the strategies each school uses to orient new staff and faculty.


## PROCESS/INSTRUCTIONS:

1.  Your instructor will divide the class in half. One half of the class will use the Nominal Group Technique and the other half will use the Delphi technique. The NGT group will move to one side of the classroom and the Delphi group will move to the opposite side of the room. Both the NGT and the Delphi large groups will subdivide into two or three smaller groups (as directed by your instructor).

2.  To select a group leader for each NGT group and each Delphi group your instructor will write a down four (or six) numbers between 1 and 50 (each number on a separate small piece of paper) and hand the papers to a student. Your instructor will then ask the members of each small group in turn to guess a number between 1 and 50. Your instructor will ask the student to hand back one of the pieces of paper each time he or she approaches a new group. The person who guesses the number closest to the number the instructor has written on that piece of paper will be the leader for that group.

3.  Your instructor will distribute additional handouts to appropriate recipients. Each group will follow the guidelines provided by its leader.

4.  The leader of each group will raise his or her hand to indicate to the instructor that the group has finished its task. After all groups have completed their task, compare the recommendations arising from each decision process.


## DEBRIEFING:

1.  Discuss the experience of using each decision making/problem solving technique.

2.    In what way was this an "artificial" demonstration of the Delphi technique?

3.    Which groups finished first? Which group produced the highest quality solutions to the problem?

4.    Discuss the advantages and disadvantages of using each technique in work organizations. What kinds of problems would seem to be most appropriate for the NGT technique? What kinds of problems would be best suited to the Delphi technique?

**FOLLOW-UP ACTIVITIES:**

1.    Meet with an HR professional in your college or university to discuss his or her use of different group decision making/problem solving techniques.

2.    Invite a college or university HR professional to meet with your class to evaluate the recommendations made by the groups or write a brief report to the head of HR in which you outline the processes used and resulting recommendations.

# REFERENCES:

1.   Greenberg, J., Baron, R.A., Sales, C.A., and Owen, F.A. (2000). *Behaviour in Organizations.* Second Canadian Edition. Scarborough, Ontario: Prentice Hall Canada, pp. 330-331.

2.   Nominal Group Technique, University of Brighton;
     http://www.dipoli.hut.ft/org/TechNet/org/eurocinet/tool18.html;

3.   Greenberg et al., ibid., pp. 328, 330.

# 43. WHAT *ELSE* DO THEY EXPECT OF ME?: SHINING A SPOTLIGHT ON ORGANIZATIONAL CITIZENSHIP BEHAVIOUR IN DIFFERENT WORK ORGANIZATIONS IN THE 21<sup>st</sup> CENTURY

 **LEARNING OBJECTIVES:**

1.      To make you aware of the unwritten and usually unspoken expectations that employers and workplace colleagues in different organizations have for others (especially for the new-hires) in their organization.

2.      To give you an opportunity to test out the validity of the "good soldier syndrome" in the work organizations of the 21$^{st}$ century.

3.      To help you to learn a few "tricks of the trade" that will facilitate your effective transition into the world of work.


**TYPE OF EXERCISE:**

Small group activities and class-wide discussion


**RELATED CONCEPTS:**

•       Organizational citizenship behaviour

 **TIME:** 50 minutes


The small groups will typically require 10 minutes to "translate" their interview data into OCBs. The class presentations of the interview data and OCBs list will require 20 minutes (depending on the number of groups). The debriefing will take an additional 20 minutes.

196

# BACKGROUND:

Since the 1930s when Chester Barnard introduced the concept of "willingness to cooperate,"[1] management theorists have worked to clarify those expected work behaviours (organizational citizenship behaviours or OCBs) that are not specified on any job description but that, nonetheless, may well be pivotal in the ultimate success of individuals and their organizations. OCBs include behaviours that are of direct benefit to an individual's coworkers, such as the individual's voluntary assistance to a coworker in the completion of the coworker's task and behaviours that are direct benefit to the organization as a whole, such as the individual's volunteering to spearhead a new venture for the organization.[2]

Dennis Organ, a pioneer in the study of OCBs,[3] described five dimensions of citizenship behaviour: altruism (helping colleagues), sportsmanship (avoiding negative behaviors), courtesy (good social skills), conscientiousness (job performance beyond the minimum requirements) and civic virtue (participation in political functions of the organization such as committees). Unfortunately for new workers, these behavioural expectations are not spelled out in job descriptions and must be learned through experience. In addition, such unwritten behavioural expectations may vary from one organization to another.

This exercise will help you to become familiar with the unwritten behavioural expectations you will encounter in your chosen field of work.

 **MATERIALS NEEDED:**

- One Organizational Citizenship Interview Form for each small group and one Interviewee Release of Information Form (to be distributed by your instructor)
- A copy of your school's Research Ethics Form (if required for this type of assignment)
- Two transparency sheets and one transparency marker for each small group (to be distributed by the instructor)
- One sheet of flip chart paper and one marker for each small group
- One roll of masking tape

## PREASSIGNMENT STUDENT PREPARATION:

1. Before the class in which this exercise is to be completed, your instructor will ask you to choose two other persons in this class with whom you will work. Your small group will be gathering interview data from an organization in the community. Your instructor will write a list of different types of organizations on the chalkboard. Each small group will choose the one of most interest to its members and will send one representative to register its choice in writing with the instructor. In the event of two or more groups' wanting the same choice, the instructor will flip a coin to decide which group gets which organization.

2. Your instructor will explain to the class any and all of the requirements of your school's Research Ethics Committee for an assignment of this type and will update the progress made to date on the fulfillment of such requirements.

3. Your instructor will outline some "how tos" of conducting such an interview.

4. Your group must find a suitable interviewee in a type of organization for which the group is registered. The interview should be witnessed by all group members. The interview time must not exceed 20 minutes (except by invitation by the interviewee). In a post-interview discussion with your group, summarize your interviewee's answers to each question on a transparency sheet supplied by your instructor.

5. Complete both of the following forms during the interview i.e., the ORGANIZATIONAL CITIZENSHIP INTERVIEW FORM and the INTERVIEWEE RELEASE OF INFORMATION FORM. Both are printed on the following page .

# ORGANIZATIONAL CITIZENSHIP INTERVIEW FORM

Name of Interviewee: _____

Organization's Name: _____

Organization's Address: _____
_____
_____

Interviewee's Job Title:_____

1.      Please describe your ideal coworker.

2.      What are the key behavioural differences between your most favourite coworker and your least favourite coworker?

3.      What was the most difficult adjustment you had to make when you started your present job?

4.      What are two things that you wish you had known before you started working in your current position?

5.      What advice would you give to new employees about what they can do to live up to the unspoken and unwritten expectations of coworkers?

---

## INTERVIEWEE RELEASE OF INFORMATION FORM

I agree to allow students from _____ College/University to interview me and to share the information I give with them with their _____ class. I understand that this includes identifying me and my organization in their class discussions.

_____           _____
Signature of Interviewee                                Date

_____           _____
Witness                                                       Date

---

**PROCESS/INSTRUCTIONS:**

1.  Your instructor will give each small group one sheet of flip chart paper and ask the group to review its interview data in order to make a list of the major citizenship behaviours to which its interviewee referred during the interview (OCB list). Your instructor will ask your group to hand in your signed Interviewee Information Release Form.

2.  Your instructor will ask each small group in turn to display both the transparency on which the interview data was summarized and its OCB list. The class will be invited to question, challenge or add to the OCB list of each group.


**DEBRIEFING:**

1.  Compare and contrast the citizenship behaviours that appear to be most important (according to one interviewee at least) for each type of organization.

2.  What citizenship behaviours are "universal" across all organizations? What citizenship behaviours are specific to individual organizations?

3.  Which behavioural expectations discussed in class were most surprising to you? Least surprising to you?

4.   How do you think this exercise has changed your understanding of the behavioural expectations you are likely to encounter as you enter your chosen field in the job market? What "tricks of the trade" did you learn from all the interview data presented?

5.   Is Organ's "good soldier syndrome" an outmoded concept for Generation X and Y workers? Please explain your answer.

6.   Should organization's work harder to make OCBs explicit? If so, how could this be done?

**REFERENCES:**

1.   Organ, D.W. (1990). *The Motivational Basis of Organizational Behavior.* In Staw, B.M. and Cummings, L.L. (1990). *Research in Organizational Behavior 12.*

2.   Skarlicki, D.P. and Latham, G.P. (1995). Performance in a University Setting. *Canadian Journal of Administrative Sciences,* 12 (3), 175-181.

3.   Organ, Dennis W. (1988). *Organizational citizenship behavior: The Good Soldier Syndrome.* Lexington, MA: Lexington Books.

# PART 5

# INFLUENCING OTHERS

# 44. POWER, POWER, EVERYWHERE:
## USING A VARIETY OF POWER BASES TO INFLUENCE OTHERS AT WORK

 **LEARNING OBJECTIVES:**

1.      To increase your knowledge and awareness of the different power bases available to the leader/manager who wishes to change the behaviour of others at work.

2.      To highlight the importance for leaders/managers to develop and use a variety of power bases.

3.      To give you the opportunity to develop and implement an influence plan.

## TYPE OF EXERCISE:

Small group activities, role play and class-wide discussion

## RELATED CONCEPTS:

*       Bases of personal power
*       Bases of position power
*       Influencing others at work
*       Motivation
*       Leadership

 **TIME:** 30 minutes

Small groups will typically require 15 minutes to read the scenario and develop an influence plan. The role play and debriefing will require an additional 15 minutes.

# BACKGROUND:

By and large, most people have very mixed feelings when it comes to the topic of power. It definitely has a poor reputation overall. When the word "power" is mentioned the image of Machiavelli pops into people's heads. As McClelland pointed out, power can have two very different faces in organizations i.e., one positive and one negative. The positive face of power or "social power" is exhibited by a manager when he or she facilitates goal achievement by his or her group by "taking some initiative in providing members of the group with the means of achieving such goals. The negative face of power is associated with "personal power" i.e., the leader or manager seeks to achieve his or her own goals.[1]

The research literature reveals that there are two major categories of power bases, i.e., position power bases and personal bases of power. Position power bases are those which come with the "office", such as: legitimate power (the authority that comes with the office), reward power (capacity to give rewards), coercive power (capacity to control punishments given), and information power (data and other information available by virtue of the office). Personal bases of power are those that come from a person's own characteristics, such as: rational persuasion (the use of logical arguments and factual evidence), expert power (expert knowledge in a particular field), referent power (desirable personal qualities) and charisma ("an engaging and magnetic personality").[2]

Anyone in a leadership/management position should learn to broaden his or her power bases to avoid an over-reliance on just one e.g., legitimate. The old adage: "Do it because I said so, after all I am the boss!" holds much less sway in today's organizations that it used to.

This exercise will give you an opportunity to try out a variety of power bases in an organizational setting with which you are very familiar.

# PROCESS/INSTRUCTIONS:

1.      Your instructor will divide the class into eight groups and assign one of the eight power bases outlined in the BACKGROUND section above to each group.

2.      Read the following scenario:

> *You are the instructor in an introductory course in organizational behaviour. You have become increasingly aware that a potentially good student is repeatedly absent from class and is often unprepared when present. You would really like to see this student's attendance record, preparation for class and involvement in class discussions improve. After all, you were led to believe, in a fairly recent conversation outside of class, that the student would like to pursue a career in human resource management. You are convinced that the student's seemingly*

*cavalier attitude will be detrimental in the long run. You are respected and liked by your students and have a reputation for grading fairly. You have decided to be more proactive in your approach with this student.*

3.    In your small group, using the power base assigned by your instructor, prepare an "influence plan" to change the student's behaviour.

4.    In your small group, choose one person to play the role of the student and another to play the role of the instructor. The remaining group members will be silent observers.

5.    Your instructor will ask the "instructor" in each group to identify the power base assigned to the group and to outline the influence plan. Next, your instructor will ask each "student" to comment on the effectiveness of the plan (judging from the role play session).

## DEBRIEFING:

1.    Which were the most effective power bases and plans? Which were the least effective?

2.    Which of the influence plans would have worked with you if you had been the student in the scenario? Which would not have worked? Please explain your answers.

3.	If all of these power bases and their influence plans failed to change the student's behaviour, what other considerations might there be?

## FOLLOW-UP ACTIVITIES:

1.	Apply power base "theory" to parenting. Which were your parents' most used power bases as they were raising you? What bases would you recommend to parents today? Which would bases would you not recommend? Please explain your answers.

2.	In your opinion, which would be the best power bases for a manager to use and which would be the power bases to use sparingly (if at all) in each of the following organizational settings:

> 2.	a large manufacturing plant
> 3.	a hospital
> 4.	a small non-profit children's mental health centre
> 5.	a fast food restaurant
> 6.	a high tech company

## REFERENCES:

1.	McClelland, D. (1970). The Two Faces of Power. In Luthans, F. (1989). *Organizational Behaviour*. Fifth Edition. New York: McGraw-Hill, pp. 439-440.

2.	Greenberg, J., Baron, R.A., Sales, C.A. and Owen, F.A. (2000). *Behaviour In Organizations*. Second Canadian Edition. Scarborough, Ontario: Prentice Hall Canada, pp. 372-375.

# 45. MY FUTURE AS A POLITICIAN:
## IDENTIFYING THE PERSONAL CHARACTERISTICS AND ABILITIES
## OF EFFECTIVE POLITICAL ACTORS IN ORGANIZATIONS

 **LEARNING OBJECTIVES:**

1.   To identify those personal characteristics and abilities that are associated with effective political action within organizations.

2.   To ascertain if managers at different levels within organizations agree in their rank-ordering of the personal characteristics and abilities that are associated with effective political action in organizations.

3.   To rate yourself on the personal characteristics and abilities that have been identified as being key in effective political action in organizations.

## TYPE OF EXERCISE:

Individual activities and class-wide discussions

## RELATED CONCEPTS:

*   Personality
*   Power and political action in organizations
*   Individual characteristics and abilities
*   Perception
*   Levels of management
*   Influencing others in organizations.

 **TIME:** 60 minutes

The class will typically require 10 minutes to list the characteristics/abilities on the transparency sheet and then another 20 minutes to record the two sets of rank orderings (top and bottom). The discussion of the students' rankings by level of management is expected to take an additional 10 minutes. Discussion of the two handouts and the debriefing will typically require an additional 10 minutes each.

## BACKGROUND:

Power and politics are a fact of life in organizations of every "stripe". Power may be defined as: "the ability to get things done the way one wants them to be done;"[1] politics may be defined as: "the action side of power [which] involves action taken within an organization to acquire, develop and use power to get one's way."[2] While power and politics in organizations can certainly have a dark side, they can also be used by organizational members to make organizations more effective. "Power and politics are realities that mangers must understand and use, not ignore."[3]

This exercise will help you to identify those personal characteristics and abilities that you believe are associated with effective political action in organizations and to check your perceptions against those of managers from different levels. Further, you will be given the opportunity to rate yourself with respect to these characteristics and abilities.

 ## MATERIALS NEEDED:

- One letter-sized piece of unlined paper for each student in the class (supplied by your instructor)
- Two handouts distributed by your instructor
- One blank transparency sheet
- Two transparency markers - one green and the other red

## PREASSIGNMENT STUDENT PREPARATION:

1.  Take the piece of unlined paper distributed by your instructor and turn it in "landscape" fashion. With a pen guided by a ruler draw six columns on the page. The first, third, fourth, fifth and sixth columns from the left of the page need only be about 1 inch wide. The second column from the left will need to be the widest i.e., at least 5 inches wide.

2.  Label the first column from the left as "Political Characteristics". In this column, make a list of twelve characteristics (or abilities or a combination of characteristics and abilities) which you believe would make a manager's political behaviour particularly effective within his or her organization. Give no thought to rank ordering these characteristics/abilities at this time.

3.  In the second column (the largest one) directly beside each characteristic/ability make a brief note (in point form) as to why you think it is likely to be instrumental in effective political behaviour. Label this column "Explanation of Characteristic/Ability".

4.	In the third column, rank order your twelve characteristics/abilities by placing a number (1 to 12). A "1" means that you think that this particular characteristic/ability is the most important for effective political behaviour; a "12" would mean that the characteristic/ability plays the least important role in effective political behaviour. Label this column "Our Ranking".

5.	In the fourth column from the left, rank order the characteristics/abilities again but this time take the perspective of a CEO of an electronics company. Record your rankings in a manner similar to Step 4. above. Label this column "CEO's Ranking".

6.	In the fifth column, rank order the characteristics/abilities from the perspective of a middle manager in an electronics company. Label this column "Middle Manager's Ranking".

7.	In the sixth and final column, rank order the characteristics/abilities from the perspective of a first-line supervisor in an electronics company. Label this column "Supervisor's Ranking".

8.	Bring your completed sheet of paper to class.

## PROCESS/INSTRUCTIONS:

1.	Your instructor will begin the class by asking students individually in turn to read out any one of the characteristics/abilities you listed in column 1 on your sheet. As each characteristic/ability is read, your instructor will print it on an overhead transparency sheet for all to see. While your instructor is writing the characteristic/ability on the sheet, the person proposing the characteristic will read her or his explanation for that particular characteristic (from column 2).

2.	After all the characteristics/abilities have been proposed (without duplication, of course), the instructor will poll the class on the rank orderings from column 3. Your instructor will ask you to raise your hand if you ranked the particular characteristic/ability in the top 3 and will then record on the transparency with a green marker the total number of students who so ranked the particular characteristic/ability. When all the characteristics/abilities ranked in the top 3 have been accounted for in this manner, your instructor will take a red marker and proceed in a similar manner to record the numbers of students who ranked each characteristic/ability as being in the bottom 3 of their rank orderings.

3.	Next, your instructor will ask a sampling of individual students to share their top 3 and their bottom 3 for each of columns 4, 5 and 6 and their rationale.

4.	Your instructor will distribute two handouts to each person in the class and will again display the transparency sheet completed in Step 2. above.

**DEBRIEFING:**

1.      How do you explain the discrepancies between the results in your class and the information distributed by your instructor?

2.      What characteristics/abilities are you now (after this exercise has been completed) convinced are key in effective political behaviour in organizations?

3.      How much (on a scale of 1 to 5, with 5 being "a great deal") of each characteristic/ability do you possess? How can you increase "your ratings" over time?

4.      Is there a generic set of characteristics/abilities which all managers, regardless of level of management, should have in order to be effective politicians in their organization? If your answer is "no," what are the key characteristics/abilities needed for each of the three levels?

5. How can political behaviour be good for the organization? How can it be bad?

6. Are effective politicians in organizations necessarily good leaders? Good managers? Explain your answers.

## FOLLOW-UP ACTIVITIES:

1. Choose one male and one female of the following Canadian CEOs: Margaret (Peggy) Witte (formerly of Royal Oak Mines), Michael Cowpland (Corel), Shelagh Whittaker (EDS) or Kwok Yuen Ho (ATI Technologies Inc.). Do some research on each CEO you have chosen. How effective a politician is each? What evidence can you cite?

2. Choose one of the characteristics/abilities which you now believe to be important with respect to effective political behaviour and on which you rated yourself "on the low side". Make a written plan for yourself in which you outline what actions you will take and within what time frame to improve your rating over time.

## REFERENCES:

1. Salancik, G. and Pfeffer, J. (1977). Who Gets Power and How They Hold on To It: A Strategic Contingency Model of Power. *Organizational Dynamics 5*, p. 4.

2. Pfeffer, J., (1981). *Power in Organizations*. In Robey, D. and Sales, C.A. (1994). *Designing Organizations*. Fourth Edition. Burr Ridge, IL: Richard D. Irwin, p. 269.

3. Ibid.

## 46. PROBING THE LEADER: DEVELOPING COMPETENCY-BASED BEHAVIOURAL INTERVIEW QUESTIONS TO ASSESS CORPORATE FIT

 **LEARNING OBJECTIVES:**

1.    To develop skill in writing behaviourally-based interview questions linked to competency models.

2.    To identify leadership competencies.

3.    To explore the concept of person-job fit and person-organization fit at the management levels in corporations.

**TYPE OF EXERCISE:**

Internet exercise with small group and role play components

**RELATED CONCEPTS**

*    Leadership
*    Perception
*    Performance management

 **TIME:** 60 minutes

Small groups will typically require 15 minutes to develop behaviourally-based interview questions for their selected competency model. The two role plays will require 15 minutes each. The debriefing will take an additional 15 minutes.

## BACKGROUND:

According to an article by Hale and Bailey published by the American Management Association, "The use of competencies as measures of performance is the fastest-growing human resource approach today."[1] This article goes on to indicate that 44% of companies make use of "competencies-specific skills, abilities, and valued behaviors" in their performance management process but less than half of these tie these competencies to rewards. The authors view this as unfortunate since "Competency-based reward systems demonstrate solid business benefits."[2]

Making use of competency-based systems is a complex task based on careful analysis. For example, Sears has specified the leadership skills they look for in all the company's employees. These include "change leadership; integrity; customer service orientation; valuing diversity; developing associates and valuing their ideas; business knowledge and literacy; initiative and a sense of urgency; and empowerment, interpersonal, team, communication, and problem solving skills."[3] Competency models such as this one guide HR professionals in establishing selection systems that will insure that the right person is found for the right job. A key aspect in the selection process is the development of interview questions that will allow the HR professional to assess an applicant's competencies in each area that has been identified as important to the company's success.

This exercise will give you the opportunity to practice writing behaviourally-based interview questions that are tied to competency models. In the process, it will also help you to become more aware of the leadership competencies that organizations consider valuable and to explore the concepts of person-job fit and person-organization fit at the management level in corporations.

 **MATERIALS NEEDED:**

- One letter-sized file folder per group
- Two blank pieces of letter sized paper per group

## PREASSIGNMENT STUDENT PREPARATION:

In a class prior to the one in which you will be completing this exercise, your instructor will assign you to a small group (three people in total) identified by a letter of the alphabet. Your group will meet outside of class (ideally in the library or a computer lab where remote access to the databases named below is available) and search the Internet to find at least one leadership competency model published by a professional organization or a company. ABInform, EBSCO Host and CBCA are three data bases which will be of considerable help to you in gathering this information. Print two copies of the model you find i.e., one copy for your instructor and one copy for your group. Give a copy of your selected model to your instructor (by the deadline suggested) before the class in which you will be completing this exercise. Be sure to include the

214

names of each group member on the hand-in to your instructor. It is important to observe the copyright limitations attached to the database(s) you access.


**PROCESS/INSTRUCTIONS:**

1.      Sit with the other members of your Internet search group.

2.      Your instructor will hand back the copy of your chosen competency model with one or two sections highlighted.

3.      Write a brief point-form outline ("position and company profile") detailing the management position you are trying to fill and what well-known company you work for. Your next task will be to write 5 behavioural interview questions that could be used to assess the competency areas highlighted by your instructor. In addition to these questions, develop a rating system that could be used to rank the applicants' answers to each question. Place your position and company profile and a list of your group's 5 interview questions in a file folder. Write the letter of the alphabet which identifies your small group on the outside of the file folder. Be sure to retain the rating system you developed.

4.      Join with another group in the class. Decide by coin toss which of the two groups will complete the role play first. The group who goes first (e.g., Group A) will select two of its own members to play the role of the "interviewers" and the remaining member will play the role of the "applicant". The "interviewers" will be given the other group's (e.g., Group B's ) file folder. The interviewers will ask the "applicant" the behaviourally-based questions developed by the other group (e.g., by Group B). The other group's members will listen in silence to the interview (e.g., Group B's members) will use the rating system they previously developed for that set of questions to rate the quality of the answers given by the "applicant". For this stage, each rater must work independently i.e., not reveal their ratings to anyone.

5.      After the set of questions in Step 4. above has been answered in the role play, the raters will each complete a "secret ballot" by writing the word "accept" or "reject" on a piece of paper supplied by your instructor, folding it twice and giving it to the "interviewers" for their combined group. The interviewers will then tally the three raters' votes and announce the result. Next, the raters will reveal their ratings for each question and explain their accept/reject decision.

6.      Repeat Step 4. above but this time the interviewers and applicant will be selected from the other group (e.g., Group B). The interviewers' questions will come from the other group's file folder (e.g., Group A). As in Step 4. above, the members of the other group (e.g., Group A's members) will use their own rating system designed for this set of questions.

7.    Repeat Step 5. above. (Each group should make a copy of the competency model it found on the Internet for the other groups.)


**DEBRIEFING:**

1.    Discuss the difference between "traditional" interview questions and behaviourally-based interview questions.

2.    What are the strengths and weaknesses of "traditional" interview questions and behaviourally-based interview questions?

3.    Identify the key features of effective behaviourally-based interview questions.

4.    What was the rate of agreement among the raters in this exercise? What strategies could be used to decrease this inter-rater variability?

## FOLLOW-UP ACTIVITIES:

1. Seek out local HR professionals who have been involved in developing behaviourally-based interview questions. Write a class letter to one or more professionals you have identified and ask if she/he (or they) would be kind enough to answer your questions e.g., your DEBRIEFING questions 1., 2., 3., and the second part of question 4.

2. Continue your own research on the Internet for competency models developed by a variety of Canadian companies.

## REFERENCES:

1. Hale, J. and Bailey, G. (1998, July/August). Seven Dimensions Of Successful Reward Plans. *Compensation and Benefits Review*, pp. 71-77.

2. Ibid.

3. Scott, M. J., (1998, October). AICPA Competency Model For The New Finance Professional. *The CPA Journal*, pp. 40-45.

# 47. MANAGING TO LAUGH AT WORK: EXPLORING HUMOUR AS A MANAGEMENT TOOL

 **LEARNING OBJECTIVES:**

1.     To encourage you to explore the use of humour as a management tool.

2.     To give you the opportunity to explore the ways in which different organizations project a "fun" image through their web sites.


**TYPE OF EXERCISE:**

Individual Internet research, small group activities and class-wide discussion

**RELATED CONCEPTS:**

- Humour as a management tool
- Stress management
- Communication
- Leadership style

 **TIME:** 45 minutes


Small groups will typically require 20 minutes to design their web site. The presentations of the web site designs will take a total of 15 minutes. The debriefing will require an additional 10 minutes.


**BACKGROUND:**

From pain management and stress reduction to improvement of immune system functioning, laughter really is the best medicine.[1] Humour is also a powerful tool at work. There is some evidence that employees who worked with "managers who used humour the most had the highest levels of employee performance."[2]

Some companies have used "humour specialists" to help them to learn how to combine business with more pleasurable activities. Author Leslie Yerkes emphasizes the powerful impact that humour can have in the workplace: "Organizations that integrate fun into work have lower levels of absenteeism, greater job satisfaction, increased productivity and less downtime."[3]

However, this does not mean that all managers have to train as stand-up comedians. Wayne Decker, a management professor at Salisbury State University in Maryland, has suggested "that women bosses who used nonoffensive humor were judged more effective at getting things done than their less comical counterparts." Men were also rated more highly if they had a sense of humour. Interestingly, the effect of humour on the ratings of women managers was greater than on that of male managers.[4]

This exercise will give you the opportunity to explore the ways in which different organizations project a "fun" image through their web sites.

 **MATERIALS NEEDED:**

- Computer with internet access and software to create web pages
- Two sheets of flip chart paper and a set of multi-coloured markers for each group
- One roll of masking tape

## PREASSIGNMENT STUDENT PREPARATION:

1. To get in the mood for some fun, explore the Dilbert web site (http://www.dilbert.com).

2. Visit the following web sites to explore management's use of humour:

    4. Southwest Airlines (http://www.southwest.com)
    5. Skeet & Ike's (http://www.skeetike.com/index.html)
    6. Roots Canada (http://www.roots.com/ncontent.html)

    Pay particular attention to the use of humour and the spirit of fun in these sites.

## PROCESS/INSTRUCTIONS:

1. Your instructor will assign you to a small project group. You and your group colleagues are managers who believe strongly in using humour in your interactions at work. You can choose any kind of organization as the focus of your project.

2.  Within your small group, design a web page that will reflect your organization's use of humour in the workplace. If you have access to the appropriate software, you may wish to post your page on your own web site. Please be sure to follow your college's or university's regulations regarding web site creation. If you do not have access to the needed hardware and software, design your web page using the flip chart paper and markers provided by your instructor.

3.  Post your web site design on the wall of the classroom using the masking tape provided by your instructor. Be sure to inform your instructor in advance of the presentation day if you have created a web page so the appropriate Internet projection equipment can be provided in the classroom.

4.  Your instructor will give each group the opportunity to present and discuss its web page design. In your discussion, please be sure to explain how your web page reflects the use of humour and fun in your imaginary workplace.


**DEBRIEFING:**

1.  Think about a time when you were anxious about a situation at work or at school and your supervisor or instructor used humour to relieve the situation. How did you feel about your supervisor or instructor after this incident? How did your attitude about the situation change as a result of this interaction?

2.  Reflect on times at work or in your academic group projects when humour could have improved your productivity. What aspects of the culture in which you were working prevented or failed to promote the use of humour?

**FOLLOW-UP ACTIVITIES:**

1.      Think of an organization that strikes you as having a fun-loving image (e.g. an entertainment company or an organization with which you have some experience). Visit the web site for that organization and explore the use of humour in the site.

2.      Interview a manager or supervisor whom you admire and ask in particular about this person's experience with the use of humour as a management tool.

**REFERENCES:**

1.      Traynor, D. (1997, May/June). Laugh it off. *American Fitness, 15,* pp. 56-58.

2.      Holt, W. S. (1996, November/December). Attitude is everything: Management's key to success. *Saturday Evening Post, 268,* pp. 44-46. Quote p. 44.

3.      Abner, M. (1997, September/October). Corporate America takes fun seriously. *Women in Business, 49,* p. 42.

4.      Doskoch, P. (1997, March/April). Managing to amuse. *Psychology Today, 30,* p. 16.

## 48. MY SAFARI THROUGH THE LEADERSHIP THEORY JUNGLE: A LEADERSHIP MODEL-BUILDING WORKSHOP

 **LEARNING OBJECTIVES:**

1.    To facilitate your review of a number of leadership models.

2.    To give you the opportunity to build your own model of leadership.

3.    To encourage you to think about the possibilities of synthesizing and integrating various concepts from a variety of well-known models of leadership.

**TYPE OF EXERCISE:**

Individual activities, small group activities and class-wide discussion

**RELATED CONCEPTS:**

- Models of leadership
- Research methodology
- Independent variables
- Dependent variables
- Intervening variables
- Moderator variables

 **TIME:** 75 minutes

Small groups will be given a time limit of 10 minutes to discuss the criteria for a good theory/good leadership theory. The class-wide discussion on these criteria, and the definitions of the four types of variables will take 10 minutes. The model-building and research planning activities in the small groups will require 20 minutes. The debriefing will take an additional 15 minutes.

## PREASSIGNMENT STUDENT PREPARATION:

1.  Before the class in which you will be completing this exercise, review the following four leadership theories in your organizational behaviour textbook:

    *   Fiedler's LPC Contingency Theory
    *   Hersey and Blanchard's Situational Leadership Theory
    *   House and Baetz's Path-Goal Theory of Leadership
    *   Vroom and Yetton's Normative Decision Theory

    Please bring your text to class.

2.  Define and distinguish each of the following types of research variables: independent, dependent, intervening and moderator. Which of the leadership models listed in Step 1. above feature(s) all of these four types of variables? Why is this noteworthy? Please bring your notes to class.

 **MATERIALS NEEDED:**

*   One dark-coloured large sheet of medium-weight cardboard for each small group
*   Two 2 inch square pads of sticky notes (one yellow pad and one blue pad) for each small group
*   One marker for each small group
*   One roll of masking tape

## PROCESS/INSTRUCTIONS:

1.  Your instructor will divide the class into small groups.

2.  Within your small group discuss the following questions: What is a good theory? What is a good leadership theory? The time limit for this discussion is 10 minutes.

3.  First, your instructor will ask each group in round-robin fashion to suggest one criterion of a "good theory". A volunteer will be chosen from the class to act as the chalkboard recorder. Secondly, after all criteria have been suggested and the class has reached consensus on the list, the instructor will repeat the process with the second question i.e., What is a good leadership theory? Again the key points will be written on the chalkboard and a consensus reached on the final list. Thirdly, your instructor will ask for volunteers to share their definitions of four types of variables i.e., independent, dependent, intervening and moderator. Fourthly, your instructor will ask which of the leadership models named in the PREASSIGNMENT STUDENT PREPARATION section feature(s) all four of these types of variables and what the significance of this is.

4.  Your instructor will now give each small group the following materials: a large sheet of dark-coloured cardboard, two pads of sticky notes, a marker and a small supply of masking tape. Each group will be assigned a section of classroom wall space to each group. One member of each group will then tape the sheet of cardboard to the wall (in "landscape" fashion). Your group's task is to build your own model of leadership. For this exercise, you will be restricted to the variables used in the four leadership models you reviewed in the PREASSIGNMENT PREPARATION section. You must make every attempt to include all four types of variables in your model.

5.  Print the names of each of the four types of variables in large capital letters on the blue sticky notes (one variable per sticky note) and place each note in the appropriate position on the sheet of cardboard.

6.  Next, reach consensus in your group on the dependent variable(s) for your model i.e., choose a dependent variable (or variables) from any of the four leadership models you reviewed in preparation for this exercise. (You may choose more than one dependent variable but remember that your model must be able to be tested.) Print the name of each dependent variable on a different yellow sticky note and place it in an appropriate position on the sheet of cardboard.

7.  Next, choose the independent, intervening and moderator variables and continue to build your model by printing the variable names on the yellow sticky notes and placing them on the sheet of cardboard. You are welcome to move the sticky notes around as you develop your model e.g., your group may change any of its decisions/choices at any point in the model-building process. For example, your group may decide to make a certain intervening variable into a moderator variable or an intervening variable into an independent variable, etc. Of course, you will need a solid rationale for all the decisions/choices you make during the model-building process.

8.  When you have completed your leadership model, check to make sure your model meets the criteria of a good theory and a good leadership model as articulated in Step 3. above. Further, discuss how you would proceed to test your model.

9.  Your instructor will ask each group in turn to present its model of leadership and plans for testing the model.

**DEBRIEFING:**

1. Why are there so many different leadership models presented in any given organizational behaviour textbook?

2. What constitutes a good theory? A good leadership theory?

3. Which was the best model of leadership presented in class today (besides the one created by your group, of course)? Please explain your answer with reference to the class-determined criteria for a good theory.

4. Outline the steps in the research process that would be taken to test your group's model.

5.   What research publications and data bases would be the most useful for the literature review?

6.   What are the advantages and disadvantages of restricting the small groups in this exercise to variables already researched in the four well-known model of leadership?

7.   If you were not restricted to using variables from the four leadership models, what other variables would you include in your model of leadership? Please explain your answer.

8.   Does your model describe a transactional relationship between the leader and followers or a transformational relationship? Please explain your answer.

9.   What would be the key variables in a good transformational leadership model?

# PART 6

# ORGANIZATIONAL PROCESSES

## 49. BUT WOULD YOU WANT TO WORK THERE?:
## TRACKING THE VALUES AND CULTURES OF CANADIAN ORGANIZATIONS

 **LEARNING OBJECTIVES:**

1.  To give you an opportunity to learn the values and culture of a number of Canadian work organizations in different industries.

2.  To understand how organizations use their values and culture to attract new employees.

## TYPE OF EXERCISE:

Individual Internet search, small group activities, and class-wide discussion

## RELATED CONCEPTS:

*   HR and organizational trend analysis
*   Organizational culture
*   Organizational values
*   Organizational development
*   Recruitment and selection
*   Communication

 **TIME:** 60 minutes

The small groups will typically require about 10 minutes to share the yield of their individual Internet research. The profiling of the core values and cultures of the six companies and the class presentation of the flip chart sheets will take 20 minutes each. The debriefing will require an additional 10 minutes.

## BACKGROUND:

Organizational culture may be defined as: "a cognitive framework consisting of attitudes, values, behavioural norms, and expectancies shared by organization members. ... Once established, these beliefs, expectancies, and values tend to be relatively stable and exert strong influences on organizations and those working in them." [1] Chatman and Jehn have identified seven elements of organizational culture that may be used to describe organizations, namely: innovation (the extent to which people are expected to be creative and generate new ideas), stability (valuing a stable, predictable, rule-oriented environment), orientation toward people (being fair, supportive, and showing respect for individuals' rights), results-orientation (the strength of the concern for achieving desired results), easygoingness (the extent to which the work atmosphere is relaxed and laid back), attention to detail (concern for being analytical and precise) and collaborative orientation (emphasis on working in teams, as opposed to working individually).[2] Further, an organization's culture is a reflection of its underlying core values.[3]

This exercise will give you the opportunity to explore the underlying core values and culture of a number of work organizations in different industries.

## PREASSIGMENT STUDENT PREPARATION:

Before the class in which you will be completing this exercise, visit the web sites of the following companies in search of any information about their core values and culture:

- Digital Renaissance (http://www.digital-ren.com)
- Magna International (http://magnaint.com)
- Bombardier (http://www.bombardier.com)
- Husky Injection Molding Systems (http://www.husky.on.ca)
- Nortel Networks (http://nortelnetworks.com)
- The Royal Bank of Canada (http://www.royalbank.com)

The types of "hot buttons" to look for on each site are those which: 1. Give an overview of the company's fields of activity e.g., "Company Profile," "Business Information," 2. Reveal information about the values and culture e.g., "About Us," "Our Culture," "Corporate Values," 3. Tell about job/career opportunities e.g., "Careers," "Join Us," and 4. Showcase the company's social responsibility and corporate environment policy e.g., "Community Relations," "Social Commitment." Please make notes and bring them to class.

 **MATERIALS NEEDED:**

- Three pieces of flip chart paper and three coloured markers for each group. (Each group will need a marker of a different colour)
- One roll of masking tape

## PROCESS/INSTRUCTIONS:

1.  Your instructor will divide the class into small groups. Within your group, share the information you discovered about the core values and culture of the assigned companies.

2.  Within your group, using Chatman and Jehn' seven elements of organizational culture (see the BACKGROUND section) to describe each of the six organizations i.e., innovation, stability, orientation toward people, results-orientation, easygoingness, attention to detail, and collaborative orientation, identify each company's core values and profile its culture. Note your rationale i.e., what information on the site leads you to these conclusions for each core value and element of organizational culture on which your group members agree for each company. On a maximum of three flip chart pages, summarize the core values and culture for each company (two companies per flip sheet i.e., Sheet One: Digital Renaissance and Magna International; Sheet Two: Bombardier and Husky Injection Molding Systems and Sheet Three: Nortel Networks and The Royal Bank of Canada). You do not have room to write your rationale on these sheets but keep this information close at hand for the next step.

3.  Your instructor will invite your group to post its flip chart sheets for the companies in a manner that will expedite a comparison across small groups for each company. Your instructor will ask one group at random to present its values and culture summary of Digital Renaissance. This group should begin by identifying the industry in which this company operates. The group should then read and explain its flip paper summary of the values and culture. Where necessary, the rationale for including certain material should be shared with the class. The rest of the groups will have a chance to add to or to question material presented on the company. When the class is satisfied that the essence of a company's values and culture has been revealed, your instructor will ask another group at random to present on Magna International and so on until all the companies have been discussed.

## DEBRIEFING:

1.  What is the origin of a company's core values and culture?

2.      How does a company communicate its values and culture to its employees?

3.      How different were the core values and culture of the six companies researched in this exercise?

4.      What role, if any, do you think the type of industry in which an organization operates play in shaping its core values and culture?

5.      Based solely on the values and culture of the different organizations researched in this exercise, which two companies would interest you most if you were in the job market right now? Please explain your answer.

6.      Why would a company want to reveal its core values and culture on the Internet?


**FOLLOW-UP ACTIVITIES:**

1.      Write a letter signed by your class members to all or any of the companies researched in this exercise in which you offer a diplomatic critique of the company's web site from the point of view of the revelation of core values and culture. Include your recommendations for improvement of the web site presentation.

2.      Do further research through electronic databases such as CBCA (Canadian Business and Current Affairs) on those companies which particularly interest you. Include in your search the following: financial performance, shareholder relations, and analysts' reports. Attempt to discover for each company if the class' perception of the core values and culture matches the perception found in the media coverage of the company.

**REFERENCES:**

1.      Schein, E.H. (1985). *Organizational Culture and Leadership*. In Greenberg, J., Baron, R.A., Sales, C.A., and Owen, F.A. (2000). *Behaviour In Organizations*. Scarborough, Ontario: Prentice Hall Canada, p. 433.

2.      Chatman, J.A. & Jehn, K.A. (1994). Assessing the relationship between industry characteristics and organizational culture: How different can you be? In Greenberg, J., Baron, R.A., Sales, C.A., and Owen, F.A. (2000). *Behaviour In Organiations*. Scarborough, Ontario: Prentice Hall Canada, p. 433.

3.      Greenberg, J., Baron, R.A., Sales, C.A., and Owen, F.A. (2000). *Behaviour In Organizations*. Scarborough, Ontario: Prentice Hall Canada, p. 433.

# 50.  BRINGING THEATRE TO THE OB CLASS: DEMONSTRATING JOAN WOODWARD'S THREE TYPES OF MANUFACTURING TECHNOLOGY

 **LEARNING OBJECTIVES:**

1.      To demonstrate your understanding of the three different types of technology outlined by Joan Woodward.

2.      To raise your awareness of the role played by serendipity in research.


## TYPE OF EXERCISE:

Small group activity, non-verbal role play and class-wide discussion

 **TIME:** 35 minutes

The small groups will require 10 minutes to plan their demonstration. The demonstrations and critique of each will take 15 minutes. The class-wide debriefing will require an additional 10 minutes.


## BACKGROUND:

Back in the 1960s in England, Joan Woodward and her associates researched approximately 100 manufacturing companies in order to discover the relationship between certain characteristics of an organization's structure (e.g., span of control, decentralization, etc.) and an organization's performance. The researchers expected to find that there was one best way to organize for successful performance and that organizations which did not display these "successful structural characteristics" would exhibit poor performance.

The organizations studied by Woodward and her associates focused on three different types of technology i.e., small-batch production in which "custom work was the norm," large-batch or mass production which used "basic assembly-line procedures" and continuous-process production which was "automated and fully integrated" with no start and stop to the process".[1]

The results of the research were not what the researchers had expected. The companies using these different types of technology employed different organizational structures. Woodward concluded: "Different technologies imposed different demands on individuals and organizations, and those demands had to be met through an appropriate structure."[2] Even more importantly, the results indicated that "the structural characteristics distinguishing highly successful from unsuccessful companies also varied with technology." She and her associates discovered that for small-batch and continuous-process production technology, "an organic management approach seemed best" and that for large-batch or mass production, "a mechanistic management approach seemed best".[3]

This exercise will give you an opportunity to deepen your understanding of Woodward's work and the role played by serendipity.

## PROCESS/INSTRUCTIONS:

1.  Your instructor will split the class into three groups and will assign to each group one of the types of technology investigated by Woodward and her associates.

2.  Each group will have a time limit of 10 minutes to plan a demonstration for the class which will show the group's understanding of the characteristics of the assigned technology. The demonstration will be a mime and thus, completely non-verbal.

3.  Your instructor will invite each group in turn to make its demonstration. Immediately following each demonstration, one person from the group will highlight verbally the characteristics which the demonstration sought to highlight. The two other groups will have an opportunity to critique the demonstration and to suggest improvements.

## DEBRIEFING:

1.  Give examples of manufacturing companies in your school's community which use each of the three types of technology investigated by Woodward.

2. What is meant by serendipity in the context of research? What role did serendipity play in Woodward's research?

3. How do you explain Woodward's results with regard to the matching of the different types of technology with mechanistic or organic management approaches?

4. What are the limitations for generalizing Woodward's results to non-manufacturing organizations?

**REFERENCES:**

1. Greenberg, J., Baron, R.A., Sales, C.A. and Owen, F.A. (2000). *Behaviour In Organizations*. Scarborough, Ontario: Prentice Hall Canada, p. 486.

2. Woodward, J. (1965). *Industrial organization: Theory and practice*. London: Oxford University Press, p. 58.

3. Greenberg, J., Baron, R.A., Sales, C.A. and Owen, F.A. (2000). *Behaviour In Organizations*. Scarborough, Ontario: Prentice Hall Canada, pp. 485-488.

# 51. LEARNING A LIVING:
## AN EXPLORATION OF LEARNING ORGANIZATIONS

 **LEARNING OBJECTIVES:**

1.  To deepen your understanding of the "learning organization".

2.  To give you the opportunity to examine ways of assessing the level an organization has achieved in its quest to become a learning organization and strategies it can use to further this process.

3.  To give you the opportunity to understand some strategies an organization can use to further its goal of becoming a learning organization.

## TYPE OF EXERCISE:

Individual activities and class-wide discussion.

## RELATED CONCEPTS:

*   Learning organization
*   Team
*   Leadership
*   Change

 **TIME:** 15 minutes

The debriefing will typically require 15 minutes.

## BACKGROUND:

The 1990s saw the emergence of a new approach to organizational change and development. The "learning organization" concept was not new to academicians but Peter Senge brought it to practitioners with the 1990 publication of his book, *The Fifth Discipline.* Senge believes that "...a learning organization values - and thinks competitive advantage derives from - continuing learning, both individual and collective." To be successful this requires a willingness to confront openly issues that divide individuals and groups. It means that some people must give up power while others take on more responsibility. It means moving from a management focus to a leadership focus. This kind of major cultural shift can produce chaos in the short run. However, in the end, it can improve organizational effectiveness. Senge believes that "People working together with integrity and authenticity and collective intelligence are profoundly more effective as a business than people living together based on politics, game playing, and narrow self-interest."[1]

Senge's work and the work of others committed to furthering the development of learning organizations challenge people at all levels in organizations to engage in true dialogue which results in a fundamental change in the nature of interactions. His emphasis on dialogue, in the true sense of "flow of meaning," challenges how individuals in organizations think and interact. He emphasizes that "Only by changing how we think can we change deeply embedded policies and practices. Only by changing how we interact can shared visions, shared understandings, and new capacities for coordinated action be established."[2]

Talking about the concept of the learning organization is one thing. Putting it into practice is quite another. This exercise will give you experience in assessing an organization's progress toward becoming a learning organization.

## PREASSIGNMENT STUDENT PREPARATION:

1. Please visit the Alberta Personnel Administration Office web site (http://www.gov.ab.ca/pao/programs/wkdevel/doclist1.htm) which has links to a number of articles related to the learning organization. These articles will introduce you to some of the issues of concern facing businesses, government agencies and others concerned with becoming (and maintaining their achievements as) learning organizations.

2. Please read the article by Peter Senge entitled: The Fifth Discipline: The Art & Practice of the Learning Organization (http://www.the-wire.com/applewood/senge.html), and visit the web site for the Fifth Discipline Fieldbook (http://www.fieldbook.com/mainfiveDs.html) for more background information on factors which contribute to the development of learning organizations.

3. Think about an organization for which you have worked or an organization with which you are familiar. If you prefer, you may choose to interview another student in your class who is willing to share his or her work experiences.

237

4. Please visit the KPMG Knowledge Management The Netherlands web site (http://kpmg.interact.nl/assessment/index.html). This site will allow you to obtain a score that suggests the progress the organization you are studying has reached on its journey toward become a learning organization. The online questionnaire consists of statements with which you are asked to agree or disagree based on your experience (or your interviewee's experience) with the organization you are studying. After you have completed the questionnaire, please request the summary score based on your answers.

5. When you have received your summary, if the final result suggests that your organization is functioning below the level of "a continuous learning organization," examine the areas of the questionnaire that suggest where the organization is not living up to the ideals of a learning organization. Compare your answers with the description of the characteristics, strategies, and practices of learning organizations described in the article Towards Continuous Learning: A Learning Incentives Report at http://www.gov.ab.ca/pao/programs/wkdevel/contlern/continuous-learning.htm (see Step 1. above).

6. Based on the analysis in Step 5. above, identify some strategies that your organization could undertake to improve its progress toward becoming a learning organization.

## DEBRIEFING:

1. What do you think it would be like to work for a learning organization? How do you think that experience would differ from working for an organization that is far from being a learning organization?

2. Reflect on the personality attributes that leaders in learning organizations should possess in order to promote and maintain the culture necessary for a learning organization.

3. How well suited are the younger generation of workers to the culture of learning organizations? Please explain your answer.

4. Name six companies which are known to be learning organizations. What evidence can you offer that they are learning organizations?

**REFERENCES:**

1. Dumaine, B. (1994, October 17). Mr. Learning Organization. *Fortune*, pp. 147-157, quotes p. 147.

2. Senge, P. The Fifth Discipline; http://www.the-wire.com/applewood/senge.html

3. The Society for Organizational Learning, Inc. 1999 Membership; http://www.sol-ne.org/olc/sol_faq.html

## 52. YOU HAVE GOT TO BE KIDDING:
## UNDERSTANDING AND OVERCOMING RESISTANCE TO CHANGE

 **LEARNING OBJECTIVES:**

1.      To raise your awareness of the personal side of resistance to change.

2.      To give you the opportunity to formulate a plan for overcoming resistance to change.


**TYPE OF EXERCISE:**

Individual activity, small group activities and class-wide discussion


**RELATED CONCEPTS:**

*       The personal side of change
*       Personality
*       Communication
*       Organizational change and development

 **TIME:** 55 minutes

The making of the announcement, the recording of the individual reactions and the forming into small groups will typically require 10 minutes in total. The integration and the analysis of the negative reactions will take 15 minutes. Finally, the formulating of the group's change plan, the class presentation of that plan and the debriefing are expected to take 10 minutes each.

 **MATERIALS NEEDED:**

*       One piece of note paper (supplied by each student)
*       One small ballot for each student (to be distributed by your instructor)
*       One copy of the handout material (to be distributed by your instructor)
*       One sheet of flip chart paper and marker for each small group
*       One roll of masking tape

# PROCESS/INSTRUCTIONS:

1.  Your instructor will make a short announcement at this point. After the announcement has been made, each person in the class, without talking to anyone else, will be asked to take out a piece of note paper and record his or her immediate reactions to this announcement.

2.  Your instructor will ask you to review your reactions and to write a "+" beside those reactions which are positive in tone and a "-" beside those which are negative in tone. At the bottom of the page on which you have recorded your reactions, write the total number of "+" reactions and the total number of "-" reactions.

3.  Your instructor will distribute a small ballot and ask you to record (and label) on it these two totals. All ballots will be folded once and handed back to your instructor.

4.  Each person will now choose two partners. In your newly formed group of three, share your feelings about the announcement. Integrate all the negative reactions into one comprehensive list.

5.  Analyze this list to discover three or four or more underlying barriers to change that are embedded in the negative comments. These barriers to change may be recorded in words and/or phrases.

6.  Your instructor will distribute a one-page handout. Revisit and add to your list of barriers from Step 5. above in light of the information in the handout.

7.  In your small group, reconsider your instructor's announcement (presentation, process and information) made in Step 1. above. Pretend that the class can turn back the clock to a point in time before the announcement was made. Consider how most of the negative reactions which followed the announcement could have been eliminated. Formulate your plan for announcing and implementing the change announced in Step 1. above. Outline your plan on a sheet of flip chart paper in bullet format.

8.  Your instructor will ask one representative from each group in turn to present the essence of the group's change plan to the class.

**DEBRIEFING:**

1.      What were the most common individual barriers to change demonstrated in this exercise?

2.      What were the best change plans presented in class? Explain why you think these plans would be more effective than the original announcement.

3.      In what ways does this exercise simulate what goes on in contemporary organizations with regard to change management?

4.      What could managers learn from this exercise?